MW00698368

AND THEN, THE TRAIN
WRECKED

a nonfiction narrative on grief and Life

RONNIE LEE GRAHAM

WESTBOW·
PRESS
A DIVISION OF THOMAS NELSON
& ZONDERVAN

I Hope You Dance
Words and Music by Tia Sillers and Mark D. Sanders
Copyright (c) 2000 Sony/ATV Music Publishing LLC,
Choice Is Tragic Music, Universal Music Corp. and
Soda Creek Songs
This arrangement Copyright (c) 2014 Sony/ATV Music
Publishing LLC, Choice Is Tragic Music, Universal
Music Corp. and Soda Creek Songs
All Rights on behalf of Sony/ATV Music Publishing LLC
and Choice Is Tragic Music Administered by
Sony/ATV Music Publishing LLC, 8 Music Square West, Nashville, TN 37203
All Rights on behalf of Soda Creek Songs Controlled and Administered by
Universal Music Corp. International Copyright Secured All Rights Reserved
Reprinted by Permission of Hal Leonard Corporation

WestBow Press books may be ordered through booksellers or by contacting:

WestBow Press
A Division of Thomas Nelson & Zondervan
1663 Liberty Drive
Bloomington, IN 47403
www.westbowpress.com
1 (866) 928-1240

ISBN: 978-1-4908-3487-0 (sc)
ISBN: 978-1-4908-3486-3 (hc)
ISBN: 978-1-4908-3485-6 (e)

Library of Congress Control Number: 2014907817

Printed in the United States of America.

WestBow Press rev. date: 5/7/2014

AND THEN, THE TRAIN
WRECKED

CONTENTS

PREFACE

I am writing this narrative for several reasons, not the least of which is for my own form of therapy. It certainly helps me to write about my feelings, and it gives me a sense of purpose. Many references on grief recommend keeping a journal as a means to understand how you feel and a tool to help deal with the strong emotions. Beyond that, though, is the fact that I think there may be use in this for others. It may help someone who is grieving to know others have walked the same path. It may also serve as an aid during counseling as a discussion tool. At any rate, I hope it helps all who read it to understand their grief better.

A word of warning is appropriate. This is being written while the grief is very fresh, as I live it, and as my intent is to write it as raw as it feels, it may be unsettling to some. There are many books already on this subject, but most are written years afterward, when the author has rebuilt and can look back on the event. This is not one of those books. The subject matter is death and the pain felt by a spouse trying to deal with all the emotions you may imagine. As such, it likely *is not appropriate for young children.*

Before reading the selected journal entries that follow, the reader should know a little about me and Merry. We had a very healthy lifestyle in the fresh mountain air of Colorado. I was a retired army officer who continued to work for the Department of Defense as a government civilian, and she was a registered dietitian. We were very fortunate and we knew it. We were healthy, we were reasonably wealthy, and we were poised to begin enjoying the fruits of our lifelong labors. The train of our lives was running smoothly. We were enjoying the ride and thought we had it all figured out.

Most of her life Merry had spent trying to help people in one way or another, through her profession obviously, but in other ways as well. She believed in the Golden Rule. On more than one occasion she told me, "You gave some money to some people who were out of gas today." Even though her informing me was the first I had known of it, I would tell her it was nothing she wouldn't have done if she had been there. It was an inside joke between us. We were not overly generous or even that dedicated to helping others, and I don't intend to try to make it sound like we were. It was just that when the opportunity came about to easily help someone, we did try to take it. Like I said, we were very fortunate, and we knew it. We were also very fortunate in that we had good medical insurance.

PART ONE.
HOSPICE

CHAPTER 1.
NO OPTIONS

erry, my wife, looked at me and said, "It is too early. I'm not ready." I would argue with my grieving mind later over whether or not she had said the second part, "I'm not ready." My grief convinced me she was telling me she was not ready to enter hospice care. My rational mind told me she had not said it at all. The part of me that was trying to reconcile the two minds was telling me that in her condition, she could have meant anything. At the time I replied by telling her we were nearly an hour past when we were expected. I did not say I knew there was no other choice.

It was a Wednesday in January, a little past noon. The month leading up to this had been one long nightmare. Merry was dying. There was no escaping it. The cancer was so advanced that her liver was not really functioning at all. The toxins her liver was supposed to cleanse from her blood, had it been functioning, had built up to the point where she was having delusions. But that was just part of it. They told me that pancreatic cancer, once it spreads, especially to the liver, is not curable. It is treatable, but the chemo just postpones the inevitable. In Merry's case, by the time the cancer was found, it was too advanced to even get started on chemo. So much for happily-ever-after. Once the train wrecks, there is no repairing it. Too broken, too many pieces—nothing but a pile of scraps.

The admission process went smoothly, better than the drive to the hospital had. Each bump and turn caused Merry to grimace in pain. The pain meds clearly were no longer having much effect. Part of that was no doubt due to the cancer. She couldn't digest the pills. The skin patch for transdermal pain medication was of little use. Even though I was glad she had it, it wasn't enough, and she was too thin for it to be absorbed by fatty tissue.

I can imagine little that could be more painful than advanced cancer of any sort. In Merry's case, her liver was so involved that the tumors were erupting through to the outer surface of the organ, irritating the lining of the sack it sits in. It swelled to more than four times its normal size, like a very large cocklebur on the inside. It hurt her to inhale as her diaphragm expanded and hit the liver. Every step caused pain. The most comfortable position she could find was sitting up, leaning forward, with her elbows on her splayed knees. She tried that on the ride to the hospital, but with little success. I am glad it was a short drive and that free valet parking was available.

We went from the truck into a wheelchair. After a short break we made a very slow roll to the hospice ward. I breathed a sigh of relief once she was gowned and into a bed. I knew I could not have faced another night trying to take care of her by myself. It was into the hospice or another trip to the emergency room.

We settled into the room. The staff reviewed her case,

and I handed over the collection of drugs she was taking and explained her condition. They had her latest tests and the abdominal scan results from a few days prior and knew where she stood. Or rather, they knew where the cancer had taken her, what point in the progression it had reached and dragged her to. I'd like to say it was an epic fight, but it wasn't. Merry, as healthy as she was, running six miles at a time, playing golf, eating as you would expect a registered dietitian would, simply did not stand a chance.

The disease did every cruel thing it wanted. To it, Merry was not a vibrant, loving person. She was nourishment. The cancer devoured her organs like a starving man at an all-you-can-eat buffet. I know that sounds overstated and that it attributes human-like qualities to the cancer, but it is pretty accurate from my point of view. Odd how cancer seems intent on killing the very host it needs to live, blindly growing as rapidly as possible, all the while shortening the life of what it needs in order to exist.

I returned home, intending to check the mail and grab some food on the way. I thought Merry had settled into her room and was resting. One of the odd side effects she had was an inverted sleep cycle. For the weeks leading up to the hospice admission, she was much more awake and active between midnight and 4:00 a.m. than she was during the day. So I assumed she was resting, but I was wrong. I was also wrong to assume she could be left alone.

Because of the pain she was in, the staff at the hospice had started her on a pain pump, an external device that would provide a steady stream of pain medication and a bump up, called a bolus, if needed. The pump fed into the "port" that was implanted under the skin in Merry's upper right chest area when we thought chemotherapy may be an option. It fed the pain meds directly into her vein. She was also put on an antipsychotic drug, also administered through the pump. Except in her case it didn't work. For some reason, she pulled the line out that supplied her meds. Since this line led into her vein, she began to bleed. Nobody was there. I was not there. The bleed was not discovered for nearly half an hour, until the staff came in to check her vitals. I learned of it when I returned nearly an hour later. More guilt. More anger at myself. More speed, says the engineer as the train continues down its course.

Dinner arrived. French toast and yogurt. Merry had not made the choice; one of the nurses had recommended it as something light and easy to eat. I thought it was a good idea. At first Merry did not pay any attention to the food. It sat untouched for a couple of hours, and the staff took the tray away. I had tried to get Merry to eat, but the cancer had taken her appetite at least a week prior. The best I could get her to take was two or three bites of anything. She knew she needed to eat. She had long ago lost count of the number of patients she herself had counseled on the importance of nutrition, especially when fighting a disease. She just wasn't interested in food.

But then suddenly that changed. Soon after the tray was taken away, she sat up, grabbed my arm, and looked me in the eye, saying, "I'm going to go down. I need some food or I will pass out. My blood sugars are too low." Shocked, I went in search of the tray. A staff member had set it aside for return to the kitchen, but it had not left yet. Merry ate it all and drank the juice.

For a short while, she was coherent. No delusions. We talked while she ate. I told her that once her pain and the delusions were under control, they would let her go home. It was what we both wanted. We had gone through her wishes, putting them into her living will. She wanted to be comfortable. She wanted to be clean. She wanted to live while she had some quality of life. She did not want to be kept alive on machines and tube feedings. She wanted to die in her home if possible, in surroundings she knew. I wanted to be by her side for as long as possible.

The night prior, on Tuesday, was the worst of my life; at least it was, up until that point. Merry had taken to spending a lot of time sitting on the toilet. I don't know if she was more comfortable there than in bed or if the pressure of her swollen liver on her bladder and intestines made her feel as if she constantly had to go. She was having trouble sleeping and had been for a couple of weeks. Just when she would doze off, she would take a deeper inhale, and when her diaphragm expanded, the pain would wake her up. She slept only in minutes at a time. When she would wake, she would go sit on the toilet.

Meanwhile, I waited for her to return. Afraid to sleep. Worried I would miss the time to give her pain meds. Worried she would try to take them herself and overdose. Sorry that she was in pain and there was nothing I could do about it. She would hallucinate while sitting on the toilet, and this night was the worst. I heard her talking in a hushed voice, so I called out to her and asked how it was going.

She asked me what time we would be there, what time the plane would land. I tried to play along. At other times I had tried to explain that she was having a hallucination, either from the medications or from the cancer. It didn't really seem to matter which way I tried to interact. She was wherever she was. The best I could do was try to keep her from hurting herself. She would see doors where there were walls. She held conversations in gibberish with invisible people. She had no bowel control and made her feces part of her delusion, rubbing it onto the floor and thinking it was soap and she was washing her hands. The bathroom and a rug were a horror scene by the time I realized what she had done. That realization didn't happen until she returned to bed, smelling of feces. Clean sheets, clean floor, and a rug put outside for one more thing to clean later, in the daylight.

At 2:00 a.m. she was convinced there was a conference going on downstairs. She was worried that as the next scheduled speaker, she would have to debunk the incorrect information the current speaker was putting out referencing the "cabbage process." I could not convince her to come back to bed. It was very much like talking to a sleepwalker, except this went on for hours. In between the ever-changing hallucinations, I kept her meds on schedule. Things were bad enough without adding a breakthrough pain event to the mix.

Finally, thankfully, she came to bed for a while. I must have dozed and woke with a start around seven, thinking I had missed time for her meds. I hadn't. I was right on time, and since she was awake too, I put on the coffeepot and we started our Wednesday, not knowing it would be the last morning we would sit and drink coffee together. A small thing, having coffee with your spouse. At least a small thing when you believe you will have many more chances to do it.

Eating the french toast and the rest of the meal turned out to be a mistake, although one I am glad to have made since for a short time, Merry was coherent and with me. She was not able to digest the food, and it caused bowel problems. With her digestive problems and her distended liver causing her to feel as if she needed to use the bathroom, as well as the delusions, this night soon replaced the previous one as the worst in my life.

What do you do when you cannot even help the person you love the most in the world make it to the bathroom? You press the call button; that's what. What do you do when the person you love more than anything else starts to writhe in pain? You press the call button. What do you do when your spouse believes she is late for a meeting and tries to leave her hospice room by way of the bathroom wall? I pressed that call button a lot that night. I pressed it for help cleaning her. For help cleaning the bed. For added boluses of pain meds. I pressed it for help, and I needed help as much as she did.

Finally, things settled down. The room had a small pullout bed that I settled into, opening up the part closest to her bedside and lying with my head at what should have been the foot because it gave me a better view of where she was. We had placed her pain pump into an orange cloth bag with handles so it would be easy to carry and to hide the lights it had. Throughout the evening, I had made it a point to tell her that if she got out of bed, she needed to carry that bag with her. I did not want her to pull the line out of her vein again. The chemo port in her upper right chest was much more securely implanted than the old IV lines, but she had already pulled it out once.

Merry fell. I was asleep. It was just past 4:00 a.m. I must have only been dozing as it had only been minutes since I thought things had settled down. I can still see it all as if it just happened. I heard her as she sat up in the bed. I thought she must just be sitting up to get more comfortable, moving into that sitting position with knees splayed apart and elbows on top of them. I was wrong. She got out of her bed and sat in the chair next to it. She picked up the orange bag and moved it with her, so I thought, *Good, she is aware.*

No sooner had she sat down though than she was up and taking a step. She fell hard, right onto the floor, face-first. I scrambled to get up and get to her. She was no more than three steps away, but I was moving in slow motion. Dreading what I would find when I got to her, my thoughts raced to choose what I should do.

She wouldn't let me get her up. She didn't know where she was and didn't understand what had happened. I realized I should not pick her up. To do so I would certainly pull or squeeze her abdomen and that large, very prickly, swollen, and sore liver. I ran around the bed and hit the call button. The nurse and two aides were there quickly. They got her back into bed. I was of no use. My ears were ringing, I was dizzy; I thought I was going to throw up.

I huddled on the part of the foldout bed that was not opened up, in the corner. Staying out of the way was the best I could manage. Merry had no idea what had happened. Her concern was trying to figure out why all these people she didn't know were there asking her questions and examining her. I am certain they asked her for her birthday because I was amazed at hearing her correctly and quickly answer. My amazement continued as my shock began to fade and I saw she was not injured by the fall. Her vital signs were all okay—no bumps or evidence of other wounds, and not even a memory of having fallen. For me, though, it was a memory that would be slow to fade. I didn't fall asleep again that night.

I was on a mission and had been for a month now since Merry first began noticing the symptoms. My mission was to take care of her. I had years of military training that told me how to put myself last and my mission first. It was especially easy in this case since I was helping my best friend. I made sure she got her meds on time. I took her to her appointments. I made files for each of the doctors she was seeing. I tracked the bills and insurance information. I cooked and cleaned and spent as much time with her as I could. I slept when she slept, which was not much, especially once the pain medications began to be less effective.

For a week prior to going into hospice, she had needed something every two hours, ether an added pain pill, an enema, a blood thinner, or an antacid tablet. The pain meds caused constipation. The cancer caused blood clots and swelling of her feet and legs. Trying to digest all those pills while her pancreas and liver were failing more all the time caused stomach upset and more pain. My efforts to take care of her were failing. I knew that on Tuesday, the night prior to her going into hospice. In military terms, my position was overwhelmed and untenable. I had no choice but to call for reinforcements and move to an alternate fighting position.

On this Thursday morning, I was shell-shocked from the events of the two days prior. I was no longer effective. That same military training told me I needed sleep. I stayed at the hospital until after meeting with the doctor and the oncoming shift. The decision was made to try a different antipsychotic drug in addition to the one already being used.

I was glad when the offer came to have a staff volunteer sit with Merry for a few hours. Jutta arrived around 9:00 a.m. She was amazing. She held Merry's hand and talked to her. She washed her and put lotion on her.

Merry, on the other hand, was declining. She refused food and only took a couple of sips of cooled-off coffee. She was mostly unconscious, but she did manage to smile at Jutta. I left. I had been "properly relieved."

Back to the hospital around 3:00 p.m. after a nap, a shower, a couple of phone calls, and e-mails to notify friends and family of her condition and to have them start travel plans if they wanted to see her to say good-bye. Merry was now on a catheter. She was only semi-conscious. She didn't eat or drink all day except for a few sips of water.

The weather was not cooperating. A snowstorm was going to delay her brother. A different storm was delaying my sister. Merry's cousin, more like a sister, was on her way and expected to arrive tomorrow. Her closest friends were both traveling, one for work, the other on vacation, but they were changing plans as quickly as possible.

I started informing our neighbors and local friends by phone and e-mail. Now was the time to say farewell to Merry. We were truly in "hospice." No more thinking this was just a stay long enough to get the pain and the delusions under control and a return home for a few weeks (months hopefully) as this ran its course, before she died. No. None of that. No more weeks or months, now only a matter of days. The focus was on keeping her comfortable, clean, and cared for until the time came. Merry's wish had always been to not take steps to prolong her life, if there was no quality to it. She saw that as just prolonging suffering. She had put that in writing in her living will and had informed her oncologist of it. Making this decision was easy for her. It was what she wanted.

Carrying out that wish was not so easy for me. My rational mind told me this was what she wanted and what I would want if the positions were reversed. My less-than-rational mind wanted to wake her and try to talk to her. The rational side argued that doing so would only cause her pain and reminded me that she was no longer capable of conversation. I reminded myself that she knew I loved her. I reminded myself that this was her wish. I was certain we were doing all we could and should do for her. *But* there was still guilt. Guilt that I couldn't do more. I told myself that Merry, the Merry I knew, had already departed. Only her shell remained. But my mission continued. Even though it was just her shell, it was still hers and I would make sure that it was cared for.

It was a better night than either of the two previous. Merry slept most of it. The three or four times she was awake she was not aware of her surroundings. She still recognized me, even in her semi-conscious state, but I seemed to become part of her delusion/dream/hallucination. She did not rejoin me in the real world. She needed a couple of extra doses of the pain meds and the antipsychotic during the night. Her most active time continued to be between 2:00 and 4:00 a.m.

I spent much of the night on the small sofa. I did not pull it out; I just piled up pillows so I could sit and watch her. I cried a lot. I remembered waiting for my mother to die in an intensive care ward from a brain embolism.

I remembered sitting with Merry as her mother lay dying after a stroke. It was winter then too. The family and friends were in with her for days as the machines helped her breathe and pumped her heart. She hung on, and it looked like she was going to live for several more days. The family decided that not everyone needed to stay all the time, so all but one left, Merry and me included. Her mom passed that night. Merry carried the guilt since then of having left her side in her final hours. But I think her mom just couldn't leave while her family was there with her.

The night passed, and around 5:30 Merry was restless again. Another hallucination? Pain? A little of both, judging by appearances and sounds. Time to call the nurse again and start Friday.

CHAPTER 2.
ON MISSION

.

A new shift of staff was on duty, not the ones who had been there when Merry was admitted on Wednesday or the ones on duty Thursday. With the shift change came some confusion over the antipsychotic medications. The added drug, the one that was working best, was not thought to be in the doctor's orders. I asked the nurse—probably too forcefully—to check again. I also asked if someone could sit with Merry today for a few hours.

A volunteer arrived around 10:00 a.m. to do that. In my haste to leave, at least my guilt-ridden mind told me so, I did not make sure she fully understood Merry's condition. I departed home to nap, shower, check the mail, and begin making the calls to coordinate the funeral. Merry wanted her burial to be as "green" as possible. She had put that wish into her living will. My mission was to see that she had one. No embalming, as that puts toxic chemical into the soil. A plain wood, unfinished casket with as little metal as possible. Cremation and all the carbon and greenhouse gases it produces were out of the question. Likewise, any sort of vault or crypt was also out. Nothing that wouldn't deteriorate, except a headstone. I got lucky on the second funeral home I called. They were willing to do the green funeral and had experience at it. They passed me the contact info for the cemetery they had used before so I could find plots.

Back to the hospital to find Merry seemed to be in pain. Wriggling and groaning. A few friends had stopped by while I was gone, and maybe that distracted the staff from making sure she was pain free. Maybe they thought she should be more awake for their visits. Maybe the lack of the second antipsychotic drug was causing her to have bad dreams. It was unacceptable. Once again, I was failing at my mission. Except this time I knew how to fix it.

Thirty years of working with soldiers has given me a well-honed ability to be very direct. I employed that art with the nurse to its fullest. Merry was immediately given a bolus of the pain meds. The issue over the antipsychotic medication was cleared up with a phone call. Merry could have the drug scheduled once every twelve hours and as often as every thirty minutes in between if needed.

The chaplain was sent to visit me and Merry. Several of the caregivers made it a point to stop by and see how we were doing. Jutta, the volunteer who had sat with Merry the day prior, stopped by. Merry seemed to recognize her voice and gave a smile. Visitors continued to stop in, most just long enough to say how sorry they were and to drop off a card or flowers. I tried to comfort them as much as I could. They wanted to comfort me, but I couldn't let them. My mission was to take care of Merry. I couldn't do that if I let my emotions overwhelm me.

The weather continued to wreak havoc on travel plans for friends and family. Only Merry's cousin would make it in today, and at least one of her connections had been delayed. The rest could not arrive until Saturday or Sunday. Local friends were asking what they could do. I was at a loss to answer them. I asked one to meet Merry's cousin at the airport and bring her to the hospital. The friend spent five hours at the airport doing so, while the cousin's flights were delayed and changed.

Others decided food and cooking should not be a worry, so they set a cooler at the top of my driveway and spread the word to drop off frozen meals. It was midnight on Friday when Merry's cousin arrived at the hospice room. By then, Merry had started Cheyne-Stokes respiration, an indication that her remaining time was very short. Her cousin wanted to spend time with her, having grown up together as close as sisters. I didn't see the need for both of us to be there, so I left to try once again for some sleep, expecting a long day tomorrow.

At a quarter before six, my alarm went off and I headed for the shower. I wanted to get back to the hospital early because I knew Merry's cousin must be worn out from travel and spending the night there. The phone rang just as I was finishing getting dressed. Merry passed away at 6:05 a.m. on Saturday.

I arrived at the hospital and was met by the nurse. She told me to take as long as I need with Merry. It all moved so slowly. I didn't want to go into the room. I didn't want to see Merry's dead body. Until I went in and saw her. Then it all hit me. Then the train wrecked, and from an emotional standpoint, I was in the middle of it. Suddenly I was surrounded by fragments of a life, like torn, sharp-edged pieces of metal. Each piece cut when you touched it, and you had to touch each one. There was no avoiding them. Here is a coffee cup, now a painful memory of those Saturday morning lay-ins where we would sip coffee together and plan our day.

The railroad that was our life together had run smoothly. Each workday, oddly enough, began with the alarm at 6:05. The train whistled as it pulled out of the station. Life, routine, vacations, friends, family, work, hobbies, and adventures were all just stops along the way for our train. I saw all that in a rubble pile strewn around me.

I don't know what I am supposed to do now, in the larger sense. How am I supposed to live now that everything is destroyed? I miss her. I am scared. I am profoundly sad.

But I knew my mission was not yet done. I had to make sure her wishes were carried out. I chose to focus on doing those things that still needed to be done for her: the green funeral, charity donations, family and friends arriving, the work of trying to inform anyone who would want to know, and helping everyone find a way to remember Merry in the way she wanted, as a vibrant, feisty person. Shock set in.

The great thing about emotional shock is that it numbs you. You can function and interact, but you really are not there, not connected emotionally to your surroundings. It allows you to continue and not just curl up in the fetal position and cry. Note that it doesn't stop you from curling up and crying; I did that even though I was in shock. Just that the numbness keeps that from being your only activity. It allowed me to pass the funeral information to the hospice staff. It allowed me to pack up Merry's things and take them home. It allowed me to begin making the phone calls and sending the black e-mails that relayed the word that Merry had died.

That Saturday is mostly a blank. I remembered Merry's cousin was at my house. My brother was there, and I was there. At some point I excused myself, saying I wanted to go take a nap. I didn't sleep. Who could? Instead, I allowed the numbness to be replaced with sadness and I cried. I cried for Merry. I cried for me. I cried about how cruel the disease had been. I cried in fear of what would happen next. I cried from guilt. I cried at the thought that nothing in my life would ever be the same again. In the end, it didn't matter how much I cried or for what reason. She was gone. That thought brought the numbness back. I remember going to the airport and picking up my sister. Neither of us cried. It seems the shock hits everyone the same way, making them numb.

Friends and family arrived later that night and on Sunday. By the evening, my house was crowded and I was thankful that local friends had set up the food cooler and had dropped off casseroles. I left the kitchen to the visitors. In this age of instant communication, e-mail, texts, cell phones, and Facebook, I focused on responding to the people who were either making plans to come for the funeral, sharing condolences, or wanting to know what they could do to help me. I had access to all of Merry's accounts, and that allowed me to share the sad news with everyone she was connected with.

Everyone at the house was either a close friend or family. They all knew Merry and knew the last thing would want was for them to be sad or feel pity for her. So we celebrated. We told stories of Merry from childhood onward. We laughed, and yes, at times we cried and then toasted the memory and moved to the next one. Some may think this an odd thing to do, but it felt right to all of us. Had Merry been religious, I suppose we would have all prayed and worshiped together. In the end, what matters is that we all began the grieving process.

I had to take some time to talk with Merry's closest friends. They had wanted to come visit her as soon as they learned of her cancer diagnosis. Merry had put on a brave face and told them to wait and come later. She had assured them there was time, and she had believed, as did I, that there was. Statistically, there should have been. But there wasn't. It fell to me, or maybe more accurately, I felt the need to explain why she had not wanted them to immediately visit her. The answer was very simple: she did not want them to see the condition she was in, losing ground each day to the pain and the side-effects. She wanted them to remember her as they had each last seen her—alive, spirited, and feisty.

We all cried as I tried to explain her condition and how it had deteriorated in just over a month. I hoped they really did understand that she had wanted to see them as badly as they had wanted to see her. We all wish it had turned out differently, that somehow Merry would have had the chance to say good-bye and that they could have said good-bye to her. I don't know if I could have done anything to have affected that. I do know I feel guilty. Deservedly or not, I feel guilty for not doing something that would have given them another visit with her and she with them. My rational mind, though, knows there is no changing how it played out. I had no way of knowing the timeline the disease was dragging her along. She and the doctors didn't either. At the end of our talk, they all said they understood.

Monday was another blur. I spent most of Sunday night editing and posting a YouTube video as a tribute to Merry. Her desire to be remembered as she had spent her life, a true citizen of the world, visiting, meeting, learning, and helping people along the way, was my motivation, partly driven by the talk with her friends. The video, titled "Merry Travels," did a good job capturing her personality. In it is seven minutes of Merry as she mugged in front of some of the world's best-known sites: the Vatican, Niagara Falls, the Grand Canyon, the Washington Monument, a volcano in the Caribbean, a canal in Venice, on the beach in Mexico, and the list goes on.

Compiling that video was time well spent. I posted it to all of her social media sites and decided to show it at her funeral. But mostly it was a chance for me to spend time remembering her as she was when we had visited all those places. That video, those memories, and being able to share that view of Merry with all of here friends and family helped erase some of the nightmare the days leading up to her death had been in my mind. I went on, numb as I was, to meet with the funeral home and the cemetery that day. I continued my mission to see that Merry's wishes were met, to see to it that the last details of her life were put into order.

I soldiered on, in shock and numb. The funeral was set for 2:00 p.m. on Wednesday. I picked out a green coffin and made plans for the service. I needed to write an obit

ASAP to go into tomorrow's paper. Also need to provide an outline for the funeral handout ASAP. I chose a peaceful, shaded hillside in the old part of the cemetery with two plots. Then I headed over to the monument company. I wanted nothing too elaborate, but still something as unique as she was. Then I went back to do the writing in order to get it to the funeral home so they could get it into the paper and finalize the flyer. Maybe other people are better prepared than I was for this. I had no prewritten obituary. I had no special poem or writing identified for the flyer. I didn't have photos picked out for either the obit or the flyer. But I did know what I thought Merry would want. I managed to meet the deadlines.

Tuesday's paper had the obituary just as I had imagined it, with a small photo of Merry with one of her playful expressions. It included the usual info on life and a listing of the names of those she left behind, as well as information on the service, including the fact that it would be green, and where to send donations in lieu of flowers. I picked up extra copies of the full paper for me, but I'm not sure why. At the time, I thought I needed them.

Much of Tuesday was spent preparing for the service scheduled for the next day. Luckily I had a suit that was pressed. That was another thing I had not thought about prior. Probably could have been one of those things someone else, one of those people who say, "If there is anything you need, just let me know," could have taken care of.

Another of those was coordinating for people to say a few words. "Is there anything I can do?" "Yes, you can prepare some remarks to say at the service." It was planned to be a remembrance service, not a typical "minister delivers a few comforting words, some sad music plays, and the pallbearers carry out the coffin." None of those actions were planned. Classical music was to be played. No minister, just friends and family telling how they remember Merry and starting all of their remarks the same way, "I remember Merry," and then going on to say whatever they wanted. No pallbearers. In fact, there were no handles on the coffin, and it was not open for viewing. No embalming, and burial would be in a simple burial shroud.

I wrote out my remarks and wrote out and went through the details of the service with the funeral director. We rehearsed. I did have the forethought to have a friend ready in the wings to take over my planned parts of the service if I found I couldn't do it. If I found the emotion would not allow me to.

It is a terrifying thing to stand up at your spouse's funeral and speak. It is very difficult. The myth that you can picture an audience in their underwear is just that, a myth. What does help is to squeeze your butt cheeks together as hard as you can and make a fist as tight as you can when the emotion surges. I squeezed; I gripped the podium; I took deep breaths when I could. I managed to get through my planned remarks, thanking those gathered for their support and comfort, asking them to support me further during this remembrance service by telling how they remembered Merry, and then I told a few stories of how Merry always loved to take road trips and how she was always ready to make a new friend. Then we asked that anyone who would, to stand and tell how they remembered her.

The service had been planned to take an hour, but an hour and a half later the stories finished. I was so thankful so many had been willing to share their memories. I was awed. My spirit was lifted. They all got it. They all understood what she had wanted, and they loved her enough to do it. She wanted, I wanted, what everyone wants: to be remembered. "I remember Merry." I will always remember Merry.

CHAPTER 3.
ONWARD TO WHEREVER, WHENEVER

gave notice at work. I had not gone into my office since Merry was diagnosed. I used all my vacation time. My boss very generously gave me leave without pay and offered to hold my position open for as long as I needed before I could return. But, and intending no disrespect to my coworkers, I couldn't return. I can't really explain why, except that I found the idea offensive. How could I go back to something as normal as work when nothing was normal? The very idea felt as nonsensical as thinking you could walk into a movie you were watching from the audience. Surreal, outside the rules of reality. My reality is the one where Merry is dead, and I wish it were not so, in my reality I am trying to make sense of my life and learn how to live it without her. Not the world where everyone was neatly dressed sitting in their cubicles working and talking about the day's latest headline from the news or telling stories of their happy lives. Deadlines, reports, strategies, e-mails, meetings (especially meetings) all seemed so very unimportant. So what? Not to mention that my mental focus was not that good anymore. It just wasn't. My mind seemed tired and distracted. All that mental remodeling took a toll.

In my case, the decision to quit work was not as dire as it is for most. I have my army retirement and savings to fall back on. Had we known our future together was destined to be so short, we would have spent it all on travel, wine, and adventures, even though we did more traveling than most and had adventures that ranged from SCUBA diving in the Red Sea, hiking on the Great Wall, and seeing Europe on several occasions. I would have left my job and adventured with Merry every day, even knowing that each memory would become painful in my grief.

I do not know what I would have done if I had to go back to work. Maybe for some jobs it is easier than others. Hopefully for some people it is easier, more viable than it was for me. Maybe, hopefully, for some it is therapeutic and comforting to be back in surroundings they are accustomed to. Back into a routine, not learning a new routine in the middle of the whirlwind of the events. Even to me, routine had become important. Turn off the TV at 10:19, after the weather forecast ended on the local news station, sleepy or not. Remain in bed and try to sleep until 7:00 a.m., successful or not. Get up, shower, read the paper, and eat breakfast. Do the dishes. Then on to whatever I could do for the day, and in between, don't forget to water the house plants. There's too much loss already without seeing a withering houseplant each day.

I am still trying to figure out how to respond to well-meaning friends when they ask how I am doing. The honest answer is that I don't know. There are days I pass through all of the stages of grief, from denial to acceptance. There are days I feel like it all just happened. There are minutes

that feel like hours of intense sadness, guilt, anger, fear—
take your pick. How do I go to a friend's house and have
dinner with the family without feeling as if I've stepped
into some movie or a *Leave It to Beaver* rerun? What do
I do if I have a grief surge and fall apart in the middle
of dinner when I recall how Merry would have cooked
something or when the conversation hits on a memory?
Sobbing and leaving the room mid-dinner is not proper
action for guests. The hosts tend to think it resulted from
something they did or didn't do. Apologies all around
don't really help. Honest explanations are very difficult
on both sides: "Sorry, I just miss Merry very much and
sometimes memories or actions bring all of the emotions
to the surface at once in a rush. No, really, the dinner was
excellent, it was nothing you did. Sorry if I scared your
children." Yes, grown men do cry.

It is two months and a week since Merry died. Most
of my mission to see that all of the things she would want
done are done, are completed. That thought makes me sad
and a little scared. I don't know what I am supposed to
do next. I don't know who I am now. Should I start to
feel better by now? There does not seem to be any sort of
"grief timeline." No schedule that indicates where you are
in the grieving process. One of the pamphlets from the
hospice describes grieving as being "on a journey into the
unknown, further complicated by the uncertainty of the
arrival time." I think that is almost accurate. I would only
add that you have no way of turning back on this journey,
and it is not a journey you chose to make. Use friends like a
wanderer uses a walking stick: lean on them whenever you

can. Do whatever it takes to make it through, to Wherever, Whenever. That's the mission now.

The grief surges continue. Anything can trigger them, from grocery shopping to hearing a song on the radio. They are like picking up one of those hot, sharp pieces of train wreckage or stumbling over one, shin-first. One second everything is pretty much normal, the next is tear-filled.

I cannot sing. Not that I ever had a good singing voice, but now it is different. I can't even do my usual out-of-tune, off-tempo, off-key singing, regardless of whether it is a hymn or classic rock song. Of course sad songs are the worst, but the thing is that almost anytime I sing, it reminds me of Merry. Either how she would join in, also off key and often with made-up words, or how she would tease me about my vocal shortcomings. But largely, singing just reminds me of how happy I used to be. We would sing in the car during our road trips. Yes, I will admit it, I even sang in the shower. We always had music to provide a soundtrack for our life, or at least background noise. Now I listen to music a lot louder, and sometimes I cry as I move one of those pieces of memory from the wreckage to the remembered pile. The time we drove fourteen hours on a return trip from Canada to home and were so hoarse from singing along with the radio that the next day neither of us could really talk. We stopped for dinner around 9:00 p.m. at a Subway and sat inside eating our subs and talking about how much fun we had visiting the friends we had just left that morning. Small talk, the kind that couples share. Not really saying anything but sharing time together across a plastic tabletop on seats that are bolted to the floor.

Exercise, especially running, helps. It may be the repetitive motion, or it may just be dizziness from being out of breath. But it helps. *Forrest Gump* has become my new favorite movie. I can very clearly see why he ran for three years back and forth across the country when Jenny left him after their one night in each other's arms. If I could run for three years, I would. I would run: left foot, right foot, breathe, feel the wind, left foot, right foot, breathe, keep the pace, left foot, right foot, think, think, and breathe. *It's okay to cry when you run,* I tell myself. Nobody is around, and if they were, they would just think you got dust in your eyes. It's okay to remember when you run. There is time to let your mind wander where it wants. Left foot, right foot, breathe.

It is important to save yourself; this I know. To save yourself from the grief. To once again be "normal," whatever that is. To make it out of the wreckage, past all those ever-sharp, cutting, and burning pieces of memories. It is important to get through it, but I have only one idea how. I have to find something to focus on, some purpose and hope that purpose is strong enough to clear some of the path. I am sure that for many the purpose becomes serving their God in some form or fashion. I do truly hope that for them, they find comfort in doing so. My own experience with God is that He/She/It is not troubled by the likes of me and my wants or thoughts. How small I must seem to the universe. My God exists like gravity and time. They are there, both God and gravity; we all know it, we all interact with them, but asking God for mercy is like asking gravity to stop. No, I will have rely on myself to save me.

"Charlie Mike"—or translated from army terms, "Continue Mission." Move forward and do what you have been trained to do.

Bicycling has long been a hobby of mine, and it was one of Merry's. When we lived overseas, we rode a lot, even doing as much as a metric century (one hundred kilometers, or sixty-two miles) at a time, with a coffee stop in the middle. Her bikes, including a classic small steel frame with nearly top-of-the-line shifts and gears and a hard-tail mountain bike, hang in the garage next to mine. Helmet, gloves, and sunglasses all neatly hang from the handlebars, ready to go. Mine are a carbon fiber road/"tri-bike" from younger days of sprint triathlons (swim, bike, run events) and a mountain bike that always seems to have flat tires. Seeing those bikes and feeling the growing ache in my knees from running too much reminded me of the fun we had.

I pulled my road bike down and gave it a careful tune-up and started putting it to good use. My knees were glad for the break. Running (jogging is more accurate) as much as ten miles a day was beginning to take a toll. Biking, I have learned, helps much the same way as running, but with less impact. On the bike you can blame the tears on having wind in your eyes, should anyone notice. Not that they are likely to see them behind your sunglasses. Besides, when it is just you and the bicycle, on a smooth road with nothing else, you can think. You can replay full days, good ones and bad ones. Yes, the ache in your muscles is there with you, and it seems fitting. A perverse harmony with the grief, the ache, and the joy of the ride. Off and on Merry and I had planned various bicycle tours but never took the time to do them. We had planned to ride on Prince Edward Island, to ride in Bavaria to see the cows come down from the mountain pastures, and had considered doing various bicycle vacations (all of them guided rides with support and lodging). Our train just didn't stop at those platforms.

I visited Merry's graveside and discussed how running and bicycling had become part of my coping. I talked to her aloud, as if we were sitting together. In my mind, we were. I can very clearly picture her and imagine what she would say. She'd be glad I was trying and that I saw that I was worth rebuilding, excited by the adventure offered by taking up bicycling again. Then she'd worry for my safety and sanity. After all, here I am having a conversation with someone who is not there. At the end of the talk, she would be happy that I was not just sitting and grieving. She would want me to live. I and anyone who had ever known her would attest to the truth in that. Merry lived life; she was not a spectator.

While I was there I planted a hundred or so tulip bulbs in the yet-to-be-sod-covered earth of her grave. I could picture her mischievous grin. I left a little something natural to keep her company. A little something beautiful was added to the world. As an avid gardener and fan of all things green, she would have understood. I left with my own mischievous grin, the first one I could remember having in months.

I bought a new bicycle, one specifically made for long-distance touring. A "surly, long-haul trucker" with disc brakes. My bike mileage per ride was steadily increasing, and I was logging more than fifty miles a ride. I was also running every few days, but still in the seven- to ten-mile range. Therapeutic or not, mentally healthy or not, the rides and runs felt good and gave me focus. I needed the new bike because I decided to do a tour. I would ride from my house across the central sections of the trans-America route established by the Adventure Cycling Association, an organization that I recently learned about and joined. If it went as planned, I would ride more than eleven hundred miles out and then turn around and ride the same route back, intending to average sixty miles a day and staying in motels when practical, camping when it wasn't.

I have heard about people who are grieving doing such things. Many write books about their adventures. Most of the authors express a belief that somehow making an epic adventure will cure them of their grief. I think they all use a lot of poetic license in their claims of being cleansed and reborn by the experience. This ride, although it might be an epic adventure, was not expected to cure me of my grief. I did not expect some epiphany to occur at some point in the ride, with the sky opening up and sunlight shining around me while birds sing in an all-encompassing moment of clarity where I would understand everything.

No, life simply is not that way. Gravity/God/He/She/ It did not organize our brains that way. I would grieve for Merry each day on this ride the same as I would if I rode around locally. Time would pass whether I was pedaling across Kansas or across the street.

I did think, however, that two things would happen on this ride. I would get to know me, Merry's widower, better. The tests the ride would place in front of me would accomplish that. The challenges of making my planned daily mileage, keeping my water bottles filled, finding lodging or campsites, dodging traffic, and being by myself for the planned forty-five days would provide plenty of chances for me to get to know myself. I also would spend time remembering Merry. Alone in my thoughts, in the springtime, on peaceful country roads, I would pick up more of those sharp-edged pieces of memory and move them from my path, hopefully transferring them from the wreckage pile to a fond memory pile. Maybe on one of those roads I would put on my headphones and sing along with a favorite song. I hoped I would. And hey, if it made me cry, so what? I could blame it on the wind in my eyes.

I picked up new camping gear and racks and panniers for the bike. I bought all the gear I needed to round out and upgrade my camping equipment, as well as the bags I would need on the bike to carry it. Tools, a few repair parts (tubes, patches, master link for the chain, brake pads), clothes for bicycling, and a few casual clothes, the camping gear, maps, toiletries, a water purifying system (squeeze bag), and first-aid stuff for the inevitable crash and resulting road rash were all packed into the panniers and rack bags. Nearly forty pounds plus the twenty-five-pound bike itself. Lighter than I expected and a full fifteen pounds lighter than the books and magazines I had loaded into the panniers when on training rides. On top of the front rack pack I placed a smiley face patch. It was the most obvious thing I saw from my riding position with hands on the hoods of my brake levers. It was apropos for two reasons: the phrase originally associated with the image could not be truer. Secondly, its smiling face reminded me of "Merry," who very much lived up to her name's literal meaning.

On my visits to Merry's grave, I told her of my progress in planning and training for the ride. I also watched as the bulbs I planted started to break out of the soil and grow. Each visit more and more appeared, but none had bloomed yet. This week I met with the monument company and they were nearly done with her headstone. I think it will be placed next week in time for me to see it before I depart to start my ride. If not, I will have that to look forward to upon my return. The memorial is made from rose granite from Canada, Merry's home country, with a collection of rocks, each one associated with Merry's life affixed to the base: a round fieldstone from her family's farm; a piece of gypsum, called a desert rose, that we found in the desert of Saudi Arabia; a fossilized seashell as a reminder of the times we played amateur geologists exploring one place or another; a sandstone rock from Arizona where we lived briefly; a seashell from one of our dive trips; and a piece of amethyst because it was her favorite gemstone. A memorial as unique as she was.

Nearly time to depart on the ride. I'd dropped the bicycle off at the shop for a thorough tune-up, hoping to avoid any maintenance issues on the trip. In my training the past three weeks, I'd logged more than eight hundred miles on the bike and another twenty-five running. That was less than what I planned to do on the ride, but my mileage and the ease at which I could do it steadily increased. The bike would be ready on Monday, and I planned to depart on Thursday. Tuesday, with a weather forecast for three to six inches of snow, would be a day to pack. Wednesday, as the weather moved out and temps climbed, was a day to check that the household stuff (sprinklers, heating, mail, plants, newspaper, etc.) was all taken care of. I was anxious to get started. I thought I was prepared, at least physically, for the ride. I had my smartphone as a tool during my ride. It had weather alerts, mapping, and an app that would track my speed, distance, and location by GPS and allow me to post my daily ride info to Facebook. Although much of this ride was about being alone, it was not about being lonely. I have friends who care about me. I wanted them to know where I was and to have the ability to contact me. I intended to lean on them for emotional support and, if necessary, transportation and/or rescue. Epic tour, life search, spirit walk—call it whatever—this was not a foolhardy thing. It was a means of taking time to heal, hopefully while enjoying the scenery.

As I packed my travel gear onto the bike, I felt I was leaving this story incomplete. That I was taking the easy, poetic-licensed way to stop it at this point: "And he rode off into the morning sun on his well-packed, well-tuned bicycle to meet his destiny."

I hated that. I rejected that. The truth was, today I was scared. Not of doing the ride. No, I was ready to do that. I was scared of forgetting and of being forgotten. I wanted to be alone, but I wanted to be missed. I wanted to remember Merry and smile and feel the warmth from those memories, not to be cut by them. I wanted my friends and Merry's to remember her. I decided to share this document, the story until now, with close friends before I departed.

Selfish, hurtful? I don't know. I was new to this level of introspection. Did sending this rip the scabs off any healing my friends have done? Was my desire to share this a cry for attention? Was I more afraid of doing this trip than I admitted, and sharing this now, before I departed, a safeguard in case something happened to me during the ride? Those are all possible, but the inescapable fact was I was afraid I was closing this chapter of my life. The chapter where Merry and I were a happy couple. I didn't want to close that chapter. I didn't want anyone to close that chapter. But there was no choice. It was unavoidable and I had to confront that fact. I had to continue to confront her loss and all it meant to me.

So this chapter may as well close with one last round of memories for everyone. A few pieces of train wreckage for everyone! Sorry about the sharp edges. The rest I'll pack and carry with me to Wherever, Whenever, on this journey I didn't choose and cannot stop.

PART TWO.
WHEREVER WHENEVER

journal entries after the bicycle trip

CHAPTER 4.
WRONG AND GLAD

The day before the three-month anniversary of Merry's death, I set off on my bicycle ride. I figured the next day would be a good one to spend pedaling and not thinking. That first day, I only rode fifty-three miles. A relatively short day, and with the exception of a few miles of unexpected gravel road, a nice ride. A dust storm popped up in the field beside me and crossed the road in front of me, demanding my notice on a mostly calm day.

Most of the days on the trip were nice rides. Me, the bike, the back road with and without shoulders and with or without traffic. I could just pedal. Focusing only on the road, my cue sheet for the day's ride, and my bike computer so I knew if I was close to a turn off. A few days had the added challenge of bad weather, cold, rain, and even two days waiting out a spring snowstorm.

However, there were three days where events I was not expecting took place:

The first was during those two days of waiting out the spring snow. I stopped in the small town of Ness City, Kansas. For those not familiar with it, Ness City is the county seat of Ness County. According to the 2010 census, the population is 1,449 and is famous for its four-story-tall

"Old Ness County Bank" building, nicknamed the skyscraper of the plains. It has nice brick-paved streets in the downtown area. There is not a lot to do in Ness City during a spring snow and cold snap. I spent much of the two days in the motel room. When I became too bored, or too claustrophobic, I walked the streets. It was during one of those walks that a very odd thing happened. A small, yellow Mylar balloon with the classic smiley face blew into me. It was a perfect match to the small cloth patch I had placed on the front rack of my bicycle. I couldn't miss it, walking into the wind; suddenly it was pressed against my shins as I stopped to zip my jacket. I was dumbstruck at the magnitude of the odds against such a thing happening. Had it been any other balloon, I probably would have assumed some child (maybe in the next county, given the wind that day) had lost it and not given it a second thought. Had I seen it at a distance and not had it run into me, I also would not have given it much thought. But it found me. I still don't really know what to think about it. A very odd coincidence. Kismet? Karma? Merry saying that she is with me? Was it God/He/She/It/Gravity or some higher power or universal connection giving me something I needed but didn't know I needed? Anyhow, I think I might have been wrong about being too minuscule for God or the universe to notice. Why couldn't such a force have guided that balloon to me? I was glad to attach it to the rear of the bike on the trunk bag so approaching cars would be greeted by the smiling face.

The second eventful day was not nearly as pleasant. But before I describe it, I should try to describe how small my life felt while I was riding. I had just myself and the belongings I carried in the panniers on the bicycle. Yes, I knew I owned things, a full house and cars in Colorado, but the stuff I had with me, the things I could touch, were my world. A small world. Every item had a place, every item carefully chosen due to the need to keep weight as light as possible, so I carried very few nonessential items.

On my eleventh day of riding, and the second one spent in cold Kansas rain, the smiley face patch that I had attached with Velcro on the front rack of my bike was lost. Forty miles into a headwind and another twenty to go before the next town, in the rain, and I look down and it just wasn't there anymore. No cheerful smile. No reminder of Merry. I backtracked for a mile or so to no avail. I sat on the side of the road and cried. I took stock of everything I had with me and thought none of it mattered as much as that one small, cloth smiley-face patch. Losing it was as if I had lost Merry all over again.

I was tired and shivering. I had sweated enough inside my rain gear that I was soaked through and starting to suffer from hypothermia. Backtracking further or spending more time sitting still would only make matters worse. Sad and feeling more alone than I had in weeks, I sat on the side of the road. I didn't bother to change into dryer clothes, even though I knew I had them in my packs. I didn't care. Not a sole had seen me on that roadside, but if they had, they would have thought I had crashed. Emotionally, I had. I don't know how long I sat there, but it dawned on me that dying from hypothermia on a rural highway was not what Merry would want for me. This "me" who was sitting beside that road, in the rain, shivering and crying over the loss of a small cloth patch was not "correct." I felt it, this incorrectness, and knew I was not responding correctly.

I got back on my bike and started to ride. I checked into the nearest motel and used my smartphone to log on to Facebook. I needed a friend. I needed someone to tell me it didn't matter. I was very thankful Beth was online and willing to listen as I chatted about the day and how miserable I felt. If you can find a friend who is willing to listen, or read, as in this case, while you vent your worst feelings as you try to explain that your minuscule life had somehow managed to shrink even smaller, you are lucky. I was lucky. I am lucky. I was wrong about having all my essential items with me on the bike. My inventory did not include the most necessary items at all—people who care and will listen.

Beth listened that night and told me I have a lot in my life. That night I began to reconsider how I took stock of those things. I began to think that maybe friends and family, maybe the things that bring love into my life are the most precious. Maybe my purpose is not bicycling. Maybe it is larger. Being a good person, following the Golden Rule, being charitable (more so than before), and taking care of friends and family may now have a higher priority. And I thought about what had happened there on the roadside. I had made a decision I had not realized. I had decided to live. I was wrong to think that losing that patch was losing Merry all over. It wasn't. If anything, it was Merry, or God/ He/She/It, whatever name divine intervention should go by, forcing me to make that decision. To decide to get up and go on with my life.

Before I go on to the third event, I want to note a few things about my personality. Yes, as you have read this, it is possible you already feel you know me well. But still, I think I need to explain how odd it seems to me that I feel the need to share my feelings with others. An introvert my whole life, I always kept my feelings to myself. But I was wrong about that. I found that I just couldn't anymore, and I am glad that I am learning to be open about my feelings. I don't know where this impulse to share my feelings comes from. Maybe Merry's passing broke whatever walls I had built around my emotions. Maybe God/He/She/It/divine intervention source wanted me to tell this. I don't know. What I do know is I am glad I am now able, as corny as it may sound, to tell a friend she held the hand of my soul that day. That for that time spent reading and trying to understand what the crazy person on the other end of the chat was trying to express, she connected me back to reality. Back to the real world where there are people who care. Where the loss of a simple, small cloth patch may be a sad thing but isn't really the loss of the memories of Merry. I am glad about that, even if this sharing has had some side effects on friends and family. Some friendships have grown. Other friends just no longer respond to e-mails or texts and have only brief phone contact. My family— three brothers and three sisters—have reacted much the same. Like they don't know me now. Or, I suppose more accurately, like they are waiting and watching but keeping an arm's distance from me. Polite, they inquire how I am doing. My relationship with my daughter has greatly improved, though. Maybe it's because she is willing to just accept me as I am. Maybe she, as a college student, is more open-minded.

I want to reiterate that my intent was not to make this about the bicycle ride but to keep the focus on telling, as directly as I can, how I feel during this grieving process. That's why I am not trying to tell the story day by day, only trying to get to the points that impacted me. There were times I was elated. Good roads, good weather. The joy of being on an adventure. A fast descent after the hard push of a steep climb. Yes, I did put on my headphones, and thanks to FM radio, I sang along. I sang to almost any song I wanted to, in my less-than-good singing voice. It didn't seem to bother the cows I passed too much.

The third event happened when I was listening to some country station and singing or making up the words to country songs that I didn't know. I was in a good mood on a pleasant ride in good weather. Then they played Lee Ann Womack's "I Hope You Dance," and I went from halfhearted listening to giving it my full attention. It was one of Merry's favorites and I heard her voice singing it, not the singer's. Yeah, I know, "weird," "cliché," "that can't be true," "BS"! But it is what happened. I promised myself to write this as openly as I can, so I have to include it. It may have been the effect of physical and mental stress mixed with memories of her singing along to the song. But to me, it was Merry and she sang, "Livin' might mean takin' chances, but they're worth takin'."

I was riding over an overpass. I stopped. Merry had a distinctive Scottish lilt when she spoke, and like me, she was no singer. I stood there and I did as the lyrics recommended and gave the heavens above more than just a passing glance with tears streaming down my face. I listened. "And when you get the chance, I hope you dance ..." There I was, on an overpass, hearing my dead wife sing to me. I may not have believed that I would experience an epiphany, but I did. I had that moment when things may not have become clear, but at least they became easier. The sky didn't open up. No bright lights shined down around me. But I did feel changed in that moment. I gave myself permission to dance and permission to start living and enjoying my life. My grieving did not end in that moment, but it changed. For the first time, I felt like I could remember the life we shared with fondness and smile when I think of her instead of cry. I was wrong in my opinion that those books about authors going on epic journeys and finding themselves in amazing ways were the result of poetic license. I am glad I was wrong. I was wrong about the possibility of an epiphany happening on this ride. It did, and I am glad it did.

I did learn three other very important things on the bicycle ride. First, I learned that I am stronger, emotionally and physically, than I thought. Second, I learned that friends and people who genuinely care for you are the most important assets you can have. Friends accept you at your worst, encourage you, correct you when you need it, and hold your trust like a precious gift. Third, I learned to not hate myself. I hated myself for being the one left. I hated myself for letting this happen to her. I hated myself for all sorts of imagined reasons. Every memory of the times we fought, or when I refused to budge on a decision, even as small as decorating the house, tormented me. I hated myself for things I thought I could have done better and for things I thought I should have done but didn't. Hate is a powerful thing. Potentially, even the bike ride itself was done as a form of punishment because of the hate I felt toward myself. No doubt the argument could be made, and I am not sure it wouldn't have a degree of merit. The people who cared about me showed me I had worth. I needed to know that. I needed to know the hate I felt toward myself was not justified. That day I lost that small, cloth patch, Beth told me, "You do still have a lot," and it was true. I have a lot to offer to the world. I have value. I have potential. I have permission to start feeling something better than loss and sadness. I can make a pathway through the rubble.

Nearly three weeks have passed since that moment on the overpass when I gave myself permission to start feeling better, and I find I need to make an admission. My feelings for Beth have grown in that time. When I started the bicycle journey, we were good friends and former coworkers. She even spoke at Merry's funeral. I am certain she never meant or expected to be more than friends. But now I find myself hoping my feelings for her and hers for me continue to grow. Yes, I am still grieving. Yes, it is still a long way to go. But there is that feeling again, except this time it is the opposite of the feeling I had on the roadside. This time the feeling is that I am doing something right, something "correct." Yes, I know, "weird."

As Beth and I have talked, she has shared her faith in God with me, an amazing, heartfelt belief that God is in charge. That God loves us all and will lead us through any challenge or trial, if we just surrender to his will. I hope she does not mind my effort to describe her faith. I know it's a very personal and private thing for her. But again, that intent to be honest as I write this, and the need to share my feelings, pretty much dictates that I write about it. Her faith gives me that feeling of "right, correct" again. She has invited me to her church, and I plan to attend.

Throughout this narrative I have referred to God/He/ She/It and described my belief in God as being similar to that of our belief in gravity. Something that effects us all but is not concerned with our minuscule lives in anything more than just a cause-and-effect way. No personal direction. An impersonal divine entity.

I was wrong about God being impersonal, and I am glad I was wrong. I have attended two services. The topic of each sermon, "brokenness," spoke directly to me. How God lets us be broken so we can be rebuilt, closer to him, more mature, more capable of leading a "Life" (intentionally spelled with a capital "L"), a full, happy life. The God discussed in those services is not like gravity. This God is hands-on in every part of the lives of those who believe. These people, the congregation of the church, are not trouble free. Their God does not prevent them from being broken. But they believe God is there throughout their ordeal to help them. The pastor described being broken in the context of pastures. He noted that although it is not flattering, the Bible does refer to us as sheep. Ranchers graze their animals in a pasture for only a short while. They cannot leave them in one pasture; it would be ruined and the animals would not do well.

The analogy, expanded to include people, is that each

of us is in a pasture. God wants us to move on to better, greener, larger pastures where we can thrive. To get there, we have to pass through a gate from one pasture to another. But that gate is brokenness. The death of a spouse is brokenness. It is a gate God wants me to pass through. But to do that, I have to first accept God fully. I am scared of that. I do not know what that means. I do not know how to do it. I do not know if I can do it. On the surface, it sounds so easy. Just let go and let God, I think is how the saying goes. But it is not that simple. There are reasons, according to my rational mind, for why I am a semi-atheist, an agnostic. To start with, I reject the idea that we are all born in sin. How can a newborn infant be anything but pure? I am also not too sure about Jesus being God made manifest on earth and undergoing that whole resurrection thing. I see the use of it in the figurative sense. Jesus' life and death represent the need for man to be reborn in spiritual belief from nonbeliever to believer. But rationally, it just seems too far fetched. If God is omnipotent, then instead of sacrificing his son, or sending a physical manifestation of himself, He/She/It could just as easily have hard-coded that desire to seek him into our DNA. Into our psychology, like the fight-or-flight reflex. A sort of repent-or-sin reflex. Not to mention all that Old Testament stuff, like the extraordinary long life spans and amazing "begetting" going on. But what do I know? I have openly admitted being wrong about some very important stuff in this chapter so far. Perhaps I am wrong, too literal in my reading of the Bible. I would be glad if that is so.

Psalm 51:8 says, "Let me hear sounds of joy and gladness.

Let the bones that you have broken dance" (GOD'S WORD Translation). More of that theme of brokenness and of "dance" (as in, I hope you dance) comes into my life. This verse was stuck in my head, to the point that I had to research its meaning. It is part of a prayer for mercy and cleansing.

There is another verse in the same chapter that I have heard recently as well. Verse 17 says, "The sacrifice pleasing to God is a broken spirit. O God, you do not despise a broken and sorrowful heart." Does the use of "broken" mean broken like a horse, where the potential is submitted, or broken like a twig into more than one piece? The pastor said that in this context it was broken like a horse, "subdued completely," "damaged or *altered* by breaking," as Merriam-Webster's online dictionary defines it.

Have I been broken by God for a purpose? Did God choose to take Merry to his side and break me into submission to his will? I refuse to believe Merry, a semi-atheist like me, was not accepted into whatever peaceful place may exist, heaven or wherever. She was a good soul. Generous, caring for others, a true believer in the Golden Rule. I believe that if her heart was placed on the scale, it would have been lighter than a feather. I cannot, do not consider it any other way. So why has God/He/She/It placed such a need on me to accept him? To believe fully. Is this gate a special gate just for me? Is the pasture on the other side truly something special?

In the book of James 1:2–4, it says, "Consider it pure joy, my brothers and sisters, whenever you face trials of many kinds, because you know that the testing of your faith produces perseverance. Let perseverance finish its work so that you may be mature and complete, not lacking anything" (New International Version).

I doubt. For now, I doubt. I am sorry I doubt, but I do. This is part of why I left the church in my teens and never went back. I refused to accept the notion that all of life's problems come at us because we failed to believe strongly enough or pray hard enough. My mother, a devout Pentecost, suffered with diabetes and three occurrences of cancer before she died thirteen years ago at the age of sixty-four. She prayed. She believed. She tried to face her trials with joy. I do not know what wisdom, what philosophic learning she gained from it though. Did she take the "wise" course of action by praying, believing, and facing her trials with as much joy as she could muster? What makes that the wise thing to do? What choice did she have?

The other choice is to give up. To not get back on that bicycle and ride on to the next town. To sit beside a lonesome road in the rain and let hypothermia take its course. To let the illnesses take their course. We have free will and can choose to not make the wise choice. We can choose not to persevere. However, Merry faced her trial with the cancer with joy, or as much as we could manage given the pain she was in. We spent her final month without leaving each other's side. We laughed at my feeble efforts at being her nurse, and we talked about the places we had been and the ones we still wanted to see. She did not cave in and become angry at me or the cancer. Yes, we cried, at times apart and at times together. But those were the exceptions, not the rule. We encouraged each other to just enjoy the time we had. To be in this minute, to not worry about the next. That helped us both to cope. Did God give us the wisdom to do that? Were the two of us, semi-atheists, believers enough to get that much wisdom from God?

Matthew 17:20 says, "He replied, 'Because you have so little faith. Truly I tell you, if you have faith as small as a mustard seed, you can say to this mountain, "Move from here to there," and it will move. Nothing will be impossible for you'" (NIV). Did we have faith enough that God helped us? Merry had faith that her goodness would continue in the universe and have a positive effect everywhere. To my knowledge, she did not even ask God/Gravity/He/She/It to heal her. I do know she worried for me and for her friends. Like I said, she was a good soul. So, my conundrum: two good women passed from my life, each with very different means of worship but both choosing the same, wise course of action—to believe in a greater good, and to face their trials with joy. Both, at least in my belief, went on to that peaceful place (heaven or whatever). So is what matters most just the belief that there is a God (or something) and faith enough to trust that God (or something) will give you the strength to face your trials with joy? Is GOD (all caps intentional) less concerned about how you worship than with whether or not you worship?

As I mentioned, Beth and I talk at length about faith. I believe our friendship, as deep as it is, was one of those divine interventions. A purposeful act by God (or something). I wonder if it was for my benefit or for hers. Was she directed to my path, or was I directed to hers? I do know this feels important, that there is a reason for us in each other's life at this time. Only time will tell what that may be. Some people may say this is wrong, I should not be this close to a woman this soon after Merry's death, but I am glad for it. I want to write the next pages of my life with a smile and a light heart. Beth makes me feel like I can. I don't know where this adventure will lead. Heartache, happiness, continued friendship are possibilities. What I do know is that like the song says, "Whenever one door closes I hope one more opens, promise me that you'll give faith a fighting chance. And when you get the choice to sit it out or dance. Dance … I hope you dance."

Going to church on Sunday morning has become a regular thing. I find myself struggling to explain the emotions I feel when I am there, surrounded by people who truly seem to believe. I stand in awe of their ability to worship so openly. They seem joyful and sincere. In these services, I find myself praying.

For anyone reading this to understand the impact of that on me, I need to once again backtrack to my childhood upbringing in the church. The Pentecostal church I attended under my mom's guidance was one that I always felt was as much theatrical as it was religious. Members would fall to the ground in spirit-induced fainting, they would run the aisles as fast as they could, they would speak in "tongues" (words understandable only to the Holy Ghost), and they would loudly cry their prayers. I was never able to feel the spirit strongly enough for it to cause me to do any of those things. That made me feel like I had missed something, that I was not "holy enough" to feel the spirit that so obviously affected others in great ways while I could not so much as cry, no matter how hard I prayed or who prayed for me. I spent a lot of time wondering if I was a sociopath. I wondered if my emotions were somehow lacking the strength they should have. I do not recall during those years, my youth and early teens, ever hearing the "spirit" tell me to do anything or ever truly "feeling" much beyond confusion, lacking, and embarrassment.

In this church, however, I lift my face toward the sky and feel such a mix of strong emotion that I cannot stop the tears from streaming down my cheeks. I cry with a smile on my face, but silently. I pray as the tears fall. I say thanks to God for all he has given me. I ask that Merry be given peace. I pray for my friend Beth, that she receives all the blessings she so truly deserves. I pray for myself as well. I pray that I learn how to accept the path God wants me to walk. I ask for the sense to know it when I find it and the wisdom and strength to take it. I pray I grow in understanding.

It has occurred to me that this journey has changed. What started out as the journaling of my grief and how I felt as I went through it has changed. I find I now write more about my struggle to find faith and less about my grief. To be truthful, I do feel less grief. Those grief surges are rare now. I can even go through the pictures of the adventures Merry and I had without crying. I remember those times with fondness. The sadness I feel is more about the fact that they cannot be added to. Maybe I have reached acceptance.

PART THREE.
ACCEPTANCE

CHAPTER 5.
ACCEPTANCE

cceptance is defined in the online dictionary as the act or process of accepting; the state of being accepted; favorable reception, approval, belief in something, or agreement.

My life was changed forever when Merry died. I cannot alter that, but I can move on. I can "dance"; I can accept the fact that she has died. But I am not too sure about my acceptance of God. It is such an appealing idea, that if I just trust in God, I will ... what? I will what? Gain entry into heaven? Save my immortal soul from damnation? The Bible does not say "believe in God and you get an easy life." In fact, it says the opposite. Just read the book of Job. Or the story of the Israelites under the Romans or the story of Jacob. But it also promises that God will stand with you, if you believe. Thats something to consider. Choose to believe and the creator of the universe will stand with you and be on your side. I should learn more about this.

Psalm 23:4, for example, says, "Yea though I walk through the valley of the shadow of death, I shall fear no evil." (NIV)

In Deuteronomy 31:8: "He will be with you, he will not leave you or forsake you. Do not fear or be dismayed." (NIV)

Proverbs 1:33: "But whoever listens to me will dwell secure and be at ease, without dread of disaster." (NIV) It does *not* say disasters won't happen or that believers won't be "broken," just that believers do not need to dread them since God is with them.

Second Corinthians 4:8–9: "We are hard pressed on every side, but not crushed; perplexed, but not in despair; persecuted, but not abandoned; struck down, but not destroyed." (NIV)

Is that what believers gain, the knowledge that God is with them, even in their trials? The comfort that God will not let them be crushed? He will not abandon them? So, if I just trust God, I will gain what? Knowledge? Comfort? Serenity in the face of trouble? Understanding of what God has planned for my soul? These are all very good things, right? But what about happiness and joy?

Proverbs 10:28: "The hope of the righteous brings joy." (NIV) Psalm 16:11: "You make known to me the path of life; you will fill me with joy in your presence, with eternal pleasures at your right hand." (NIV) Lately I have felt joy in my life and a growing sense of peace. Is it because I have some faith in God? Is it because I am beginning to accept Merry's death? Is it because of how I feel about Beth? And the biggest question of all, "Is all of it God's work? Are all three—my growing faith, my feelings for Beth, and my acceptance of Merry's death—blessings from God?"

There are two things that cause me to ponder love. The first is that one of my nieces is expecting her third baby very soon. The second is an internal question that I ask myself: "How can I feel like I do toward Beth this soon after

Merry's death?" I visited my family over a recent holiday weekend and spent some time with my very pregnant niece. She was "glowing." Happy, healthy, full of excitement and wonder, it was clear she could hardly wait to meet her not-yet-arrived child. She loved it already, fully and openly. My second reason to ponder love is that I have admitted to myself and to Beth that I love her. What made that possible?

For what they are worth, here are my ramblings as I consider these two events occurring in my life. First, I must say I am amazed at the capacity of the human heart for love. A mother does not love her first child (or children) less when she has a second one. No, her love is instantly doubled and she loves them both. When we make new friends, we don't decrease the love we have for existing friends. Nope, we just love more. So it is that I think I can love Beth while still keeping the memory of the love I had with Merry. If love was kinetic, it would be the ultimate perpetual-motion machine. Encounter an uphill climb? Just love more. Stuck in a rut? No problem, just give life a little more love. Love is free and there is a never-ending supply.

I was talking with a friend, and the subject of cigarette smoking came up. I am addicted to nicotine. I quit smoking and chewing in December 1999 after smoking and/or chewing snuff for nearly twenty years. Today, fourteen and a half years later, I still want to smoke. I have to make the decision not to use tobacco every time the feeling hits me. The time that has passed has made making that decision easier. It is more routine. The standard answer I give myself is, "*No*, I will not smoke," and because I have told myself that and stuck to it, I accept it. It has become easier to do that over time. Now, the odd thing is I am beginning to think accepting God may be a similar thing. Like quitting smoking, it is not a one-time thing. I could not just instantly quit. I cannot expect to instantly accept God. Just as I have to choose to not use tobacco, I have to choose to accept and trust in God. That choice has to be made continually, not just once. That is how I think faith works. I have to have enough faith to know that making that choice, choosing to accept and trust in God, is the right thing. The healthy thing. The good thing for me. I hope that like my experience in quitting tobacco, that decision to say, "*Yes*, I will accept and trust in God," gets easier and more routine over time.

There is a second parallelism to quitting smoking. When I quit, I felt as if I had to relearn how to do the things I routinely did while smoking. Things like driving and what to do after eating or exercising had to be relearned as a former smoker. I had to learn how to do them while not smoking. Those of you who have quit any addiction will know what I mean. For those of you who have never smoked, or who have never stopped doing something you are addicted to may find that an odd thing. But I think it applies to accepting God as well. I have to relearn some basic things in my life and learn how to do them in the light of God's grace. I am not yet sure what that means, but I feel it is right and true and part of accepting God.

I met a man who has given me a picture of what living in God's grace may mean. His name is Peter. He is an odd character when compared to most of us. Peter is near destitute by my standards, but he either doesn't realize it or doesn't care. He has enough to share, in his opinion. He spends a lot of his time in a small, poorly lit bicycle repair shop located in a larger warehouse complex doing bicycle repairs (mostly for free) and building bicycles to give to the homeless. His shop is full from floor to ceiling with used bicycle parts. Out front is a small handwritten sign that simply says "Bike Clinic." Anyone can stop by if they need a bike or need repairs. If Peter is not there, he has a notepad and a pencil and with a small sign asking that you leave a note with a phone number or anticipated time you can return so he can try to meet you.

I met Peter through a local bicycle shop when I asked if they had any interest in or knew where I could sell or donate a few used bicycles. Like most bicyclists, over the years, I have accumulated several bicycles and spare parts. The buyer for the shop has known Peter for years, and the owners assist in keeping Peter's small shop open. The shop takes in used and broken bikes and then gives them to Peter.

Since I had several bikes, I went along when the shop made its next drop off to Peter. While there, I watched as a homeless man pushed a bicycle up and asked Peter if he could fix his broken pedal. It was fixed in just a few minutes with one of the pedals I had just dropped off. It was one of those moments constructed by fate, coincidence, or by God's hand. Regardless, it gave me a good, blessed feeling. I talked with Peter some during this visit. He is a person who simply does what he can to help others. As he explained it, he was raised as a Mennonite and just believes "love" is the most important thing. He's a small, wiry man missing most of one finger and who cuts the front of his shoes open to accommodate his crooked toes. Dressed in dirty, oil-and–sweat-stained and torn clothes, but smiling, he was nearly beaming when he talked about how God wants us all to just love one another. I departed that day with a light heart, thinking I had done something good by donating a few bikes and a couple of boxes of parts to a good cause.

Being a nonworking person, I decided I have time to do some volunteer work. I have culled through the Internet sites and have done some trail-building in a nearby park. But I haven't found anything that has struck a chord like the work Peter does in repairing and building bicycles for the homeless. Clearly I have an interest in and experience with bicycles, but what amazes me most is Peter's heartfelt joy in what he does. I want to share in his joy. I want to learn about what he believes. It seems a little odd. I mean, here I am, a retired army officer, wealthy enough to not need to work and educated to postgraduate levels, wanting to learn from a man who at first glance could easily be mistaken for one of the homeless he spends his time helping.

So I returned to his small shop to see how I could help. He remembered me from my previous visit and told me he had given away two of the bikes I had donated, while two others had been sold, with the money going to buy locks and parts. We talked some more and exchanged phone numbers. Peter prefers to work alone in his small shop, so we reached a deal where I will pick up bikes from him when he gets a backlog and take them to my home to repair them. It is a start. I don't know how it will work out, but it is another of those things that feels "right."

There are times when it seems that now, as I grow in faith, I see people in a different way. I look to see if they know God's grace. I listen for it in their voices and faces. It is a certain calmness and openness in their demeanor that is quickly replaced by joy when they are with people they love and true concern when they are with people who need support. It is easier to spot now. Possibly I just never looked before. Or maybe it is like learning how to recognize constellations in the night sky. Once you know what to look for, you can see them clearly, but if you don't know, then all you see are random stars.

Peter is a constellation. Beth is a constellation. My sister, the mother of the niece I mentioned before, is a constellation. In my sister's thoughts, three things are important in life: faith, family, and health. There are others I have met who shine (as cliché as that sounds) with God's grace as well. People see the light they give off and are drawn to them when they need support, and they open their hearts and do what they can to help them. I am not a constellation. When I meet people, they do not tell me their troubles, opening the door for me to offer assistance. People, not even friends and family, do not seek me out when they are in need to ask for help or advice. Not yet anyway.

I was cleaning out some old notes today on the computer when I came across the following e-mail, written by Merry to one of her friends two weeks before she died. It is one of those still hot and sharp-edged pieces from the train wreck. I enclose it below, as written, typos and partial sentences included.

Subject: Just up for a (nothing else written)
Just up for a couple of minutes, poor sleeps. So after going through scans, lab data at out comes and the

advanced liver tumor, I will forego treatment a and
head directly to palliative care
It will give Ron and I a bit more time. So hopefully
can sign in tomorrow need
So tired to heading off

As I read and reread it, I am amazed at Merry's courage and at how big her heart was. I know it was a tough decision. We talked about it in the days leading up to this e-mail. The "time" she mentions is actually more "quality time," as we called it. Time with her as herself, not in great pain or medicated. We did not get as much of that time as we had hoped, but I am so thankful for the time we did have.

Nine days later she entered hospice, and she died three days after that. I included the e-mail here because I found it just today and because it is indicative of how it is when dealing with the loss of a loved one. There are little things like finding an old e-mail that will bring the full emotion of the loss to the front and center of your attention. My conscious mind says months have passed since then, but my grieving mind remembers it as if it was yesterday. Even now, when I believe I have accepted Merry's death, the pain is so strong that I cry loudly. However, as the grief passes, I remember the love that we had and I grin. I was blessed by the love we shared and didn't know it.

I have not figured out this "Life with a capital L" yet. Last Sunday in church I dropped a note in the offering basket introducing myself as a new attendee, stating I am a widower and asking for some grief counseling. Today I received an e-mail with an offer to talk and a phone number to call to schedule a time. In hindsight, I am not sure if grief counseling is what I want, so much as I want to discuss faith. I want to ask about those things in the Old Testament that are incongruent with science. I want to ask about the idea that we are all born in sin and must repent. I want to ask about whether being a good person, without following the rites like taking communion, reading the Bible, and attending church regularly, is enough. Was it enough that Merry will be in peace? Or does God's unconditional love only extend to the church flock? I want to give whoever gets stuck with the unenviable task of being my counselor a copy of this journal to read, and I want to sit with this person and discuss it once that copy has been received. Ultimately, I want the church to help me find what it is God wants for me. I want the church to help me get this journal to others who may be grieving or who may be struggling with accepting God because I think it may help them.

Bureaucracy, it seems, even finds a way into churches. Two weeks later and I find I am unable to arrange to meet with a minister/counselor at the church. Several occurrences of phone tag—that un-fun game where you call and leave a voice mail, then they call and leave a voice mail—have passed. Tag, your turn to call my phone. But maybe that is God's will too. This story is not yet over. It is too soon to share it. My journey through the grief of Merry's passing is not done. I am reminded of that less frequently now, but still the reminders come, the feelings of loss and sadness. My journey to find my faith is also not done.

I recently read the book *The Shack*. When it was first published in 2007, it caused quite a stir. The story is about a man who gets a note from God, "Papa," as the book refers to him, saying he would be at the shack the next weekend. The shack is the scene of the murder of the man's daughter, so getting a note from God saying he would be there during the weekend provides a good storyline. The book is fiction. The author, Wm. Paul Young, wrote it as a story for his children to teach them about God's love. I read it thinking it was nonfiction, and as I read, I wanted to believe God may have loved Mack, the central character, enough to visit with him for a weekend to restore his faith. It was after I had finished it that I learned it was fictional. I mention having read this book because I was thinking about it as I was running. Running remains a joy for me, although I don't think "joy" is the right word for it. It is more like a chance to think and to enjoy the outdoors. Mobile meditation? Jogging "zensation"? Regardless, as I ran, I thought, *Is the idea that God could spend a weekend with a person and teach him about his love that farfetched? Would God make that much of an effort to return a prodigal son to the fold? Does God love each of us that much?*

The Bible tells us Jesus walked among us as a man for some thirty-three years. We believe it. It tells us God delivered the Ten Commandments to Moses appearing in the form of a burning bush. We believe it. This thought stopped me. I stopped running and I sat on a large rock beside the trail. If I can believe God once appeared to a man in the form of a burning bush and narrated commandments to him that we all accept still to this day, why would I set limits on what I believe God can do? Why would I think I can believe God gave Moses the Ten Commandments but not believe, for example that God told Noah how to build an ark? Can I believe Jesus died on the cross so that we, mankind, can have a means of knowing God's love? I decided that for now, it is enough that I know God does love me.

I sat on that rock and gazed at the beauty of the forested trail and said a prayer of thanks. I thanked God for the day, for the chance to run on a warm afternoon. I thanked God for loving me. I asked God to keep helping me on my journey to Wherever, Whenever. I thanked God for giving me such a powerful reminder of his presence. Then I continued my run.

This Sunday morning, communion was part of the service at church. I did not take the wafer or drink the wine. I passed the trays onward and I prayed instead. I remember the communion rite being part of our church during my childhood years. It always seemed too important, too scary for children to take part in. Regardless, I do not currently feel worthy. I still have my doubts.

I got a note from a longtime friend telling me his wife has died, not unexpectedly, from pulmonary fibrosis. I am grabbing a flight to visit him. I do not know if I can provide any comfort, but I want to try. I need to try. I am taking him a copy of this journal.

My travels were good. It was good to see my friend. My message to him is and was a simple one: "Your friends are there for you."

My friends are there for me too, and now that I have gotten a little further along in my journey, I think it is time to give them an update. Time to let them read this journal again. I have moved along my way to Wherever, Whenever quite a bit since they last read it.

Being honest here; that's the deal. That's what I promised when I started this. Honest, raw, written as close to how it feels as I can. So in that vein, I need to talk about something. I do not visit Merry's gravesite very often. There it is, my confession, seemingly small as it may sound. But it's one of those things that carries more emotional import than it may seem on the surface. I started out making regular trips to the cemetery. I would talk to her gravesite as if she could hear me. I would tell her my plans and feelings. The wind would hear them and the wind would reply. I would leave feeling as if I was still connected to her.

But now I hardly go. I haven't been there for nearly a month now. I feel guilty because I think I should go more often. I think visiting more would be honoring her memory. But the truth is, when I go, I do not feel as if she is there. I do not feel a connection with her there, in the cemetery. At least not any longer. Part of that is because I gave her a green burial, as she wanted; no embalming, no vault, just a simple, unfinished wooden coffin and a linen wrap around her body. So in my mind, by now, not much of her body remains. Her headstone marks the spot where her body used to be, that's all. I have no doubt that her indomitable spirit is traveling the world, perhaps the universe, free of care and safe in God's love. Merry, the soul I knew, is not under some cold patch of dirt in a cemetery. I carry her with me as memories. Her friends carry parts of her too, as does everyone she knew and every place she went. The places we visited together carry more connection to her than her grave because they remind me of the fun, of the adventure, and of her. We never went to the cemetery together, not the one she is buried in, anyway, so I have no memory of her there. So why visit? The answer is that I do still plan to visit regardless of how I feel right now. I do still plan to drop off flowers. I will likely sit beside her grave and talk to the wind. Why? Well, because maybe, just maybe, it does mean more than I give it credit for. And because I think that if our places were reversed, and it was my grave, I would want someone I loved to stop by occasionally and visit. That's probably not too much to ask.

CHAPTER 6.
OUT FROM THE WRECKAGE

like myself now. That statement, with the word "now" in it, implies I did not like myself before. That is truth. The fact is I did not like myself after Merry died. The fact is I am much changed now from the person I was then and I continue to change. I do not understand why, but Merry's death launched me on a search for myself. A new me, without her. In my mental image of me, I see a new Ronnie emerging from the wreckage, one I like and hope will be happy again. The extent of my personal change may be best captured in the change in how I sum up my philosophy on living life.

Before Merry's death, my life philosophy was this: "When you work, build something to be proud of. Keep your head up and pay attention. Do the basic things well. They are the building blocks for everything else. Take time to build both mind and body. Life takes balance. It does not matter where you came from; what matters is where you are and where you are going. Never underestimate the importance of reconnaissance. Knowing is half the battle (with apologies to GI Joe)."

Not a bad set of beliefs, but missing a few things I now think are very, very important: God, family, and love. You may also notice it is very self-centered. When I wrote it, I was already in the army, serving as a lieutenant and preparing someday to take command of an infantry company. As part of that, my goal was to develop a command philosophy, a written "here is what I think is important" set of guidance I would follow and expect my soldiers to follow. I have followed it more or less since.

Today, however, I have rewritten my "here's how to live" philosophy: "Life is an adventure. Be honest, even when it scares you. Work hard. Be choosy. Say 'thank you' and 'I love you' as often as you can, especially to God. Go to church. Seek the wisdom in the Bible. The Lord giveth ... he even gave you freewill, so choose wisely. Know your life has value. God has a purpose for you; accept his will. He stands with you now and loves you. Dreaming does matter. It allows you to become that which you aspire to be. Laugh often. Try, yes *try*. Appreciate the little things in life and enjoy them, you may learn that they are actually the big things. Do not worry; worry is a waste of time. Forgive, because it frees the soul. Take time for yourself— plan for longevity. Recognize the special people you have been blessed to know. Live in the moment, enjoy the ride, and *dance*."

This is now framed and hanging on my wall so I can read it and remind myself. There are some very difficult challenges in this new life philosophy. No doubt I will fail often, so I think keeping them within easy eyesight is a good idea.

When Merry died, I asked myself, *What am I going to do now? How am I supposed to carry on now that the one person I had centered the plans for the rest of my life around is gone?* That question was partly answered on my bicycle journey by Merry herself, in my mind, singing "I Hope You Dance." That epiphany was the realization that I have permission to be happy and need to find a way to rebuild my life. It is very empowering. It is probably something most people take for granted.

The fact is we are all, each of us, in charge of our lives. We all have permission to find happiness. It is even embedded in our Declaration of Independence, "We hold these truths to be self-evident, that all men are created equal, that they are endowed by their Creator with certain unalienable rights, that among these are life, liberty and the pursuit of happiness." Although I do not think it has quit the same context as I have experienced it, it shares the same underlying characteristic and the point I want to make. It is an unalienable right. We as people have the right to try to be happy. The steps I have made through the wreckage of the life I had planned, to this point, have had that as their aiming point, a point I couldn't see at first. Too much haze and too much wreckage made it impossible to see it, but somehow, with God's assistance no doubt, I made steps toward it even then.

Can I see it now? Can I see happiness farther down the way? *Yes!* I pray anyone reading this knows that feeling too. The feeling that you can choose happiness. You can rebuild. You can move on. You can find a path. Yes, your grief will go with you. Yes, your memories, the good ones and the bad ones, will also travel with you. But the journey changes from one being headed to Wherever, Whenever to one of being headed for Happiness. Whatever that is to you, however you define it. The journey becomes less of a trudge, crashing shins first into hot and sharp-edged memories, to much more of a pleasant hike on a mild day, full of adventure, in the pursuit of happiness.

I think I am still the same person, but now I hug more. I am more open. I am more willing to empathize with others. This change did not come that quickly. I was very angry and sad at first. I still struggle at times with anger. It seems to pop out almost unexpectedly and out of proportion to the situation. Cut off in traffic—I may question your parentage and utilize universally known hand signals out of anger. But only for an instant, and then it cools. It takes time to get through the anger. There is a reason we refer to anger as "simmering." It is one of those things we all have felt, that anger pot suddenly boiling over.

Communion is still on my mind since the last time it was offered at church and I, as I always have, did not partake. I think I have misunderstood it. What little I know about it comes from my experience in my childhood church. That being primarily just a fear that doing it in an "unworthy manner" is a big deal. A very bad thing.

Communion was never practiced without the caution found in 1 Corinthians 11:27–29 being strongly voiced: "Whoever, therefore, eats the bread or drinks the cup of the Lord in an unworthy manner will be guilty concerning the body and blood of the Lord. Let a person examine himself, then, and so eat of the bread and drink of the cup. For anyone who eats and drinks without discerning the body eats and drinks judgment on himself." (NIV)

In my childhood, the church pastor was the greatest authority figure in my life. Whatever he said was law. He was a "man of God," and some of our pastors even spoke directly with God—according to their claims anyhow. I was a child, and I believed them. They very well may have talked with God, or God spoke through them; what do I know?

However, what I am learning is that most of what I remember from my childhood religious experience does not match what I believe now. Now I choose to believe God is a loving God, not a mean one, a God who is involved in our lives directly, guiding us, not one who sits on his throne and waits for us to sin so he can pounce on us and condemn us to hell. Is communion one of those things I was taught as part of the effort to inspire fear of God's wrath, instead of the warmth of God's love? I believe it is.

Jesus told us, "This is my body, which is for you; do this in remembrance of me." So if we are told, by the Lord, to share communion with each other and remember him as we do it, then it must surely be a joyous event, or if not joyous, then at the least certainly not a frightening, possibly soul-damning event. It would seem more intended to be a public declaration of faith, a way of saying, "Yes, I believe Jesus gave his life for us." A way of joining the congregation of Christians.

I have decided to take communion the next time it is offered at church. Writing that statement, putting it down in print is scary, but empowering. It is amazing how deeply that childhood fear is rooted. Strong enough to still feel it forty years later. Strong enough to not even have questioned it for those forty years. I will do it, but I know I will feel that fear when I do. I wonder how I will feel afterward. I hope it just feels warm, like a welcome hug from a friend.

In so many ways, communion did feel like a welcome hug from a friend. Yes, those childhood fears, as irrational as they seem now, were there. Yes, I cried. Before I ate the communion wafer, I asked God to accept and forgive me. Like David prayed in Psalm 51:2–3, I asked God, to "wash me thoroughly from my iniquity and cleanse me from my sin. For I know my transgressions, and my sin is ever before me." (NIV) No, nothing like David and Bathsheba; my sin was not like that at all. My sin, the sin I felt would be before me forever, was one of arrogance and ignorance. I felt guilty because I was too arrogant to accept that God is real. My arrogance caused me to think I knew what was real, to think I was smart in how I had defined God, when in truth I was an idiot. I felt guilt in having missed out on being part of God's congregation for many years. But worse, I felt I was ignorant. I had been stupid and blind. My guilt was the feeling that if I had accepted God and "let my light shine," it may have brought Merry closer to God as well.

I thought I would carry this guilt "ever before me." However, I know God has forgiven me. He heard me. This is one of those times where I have proof God has forgiven me. That proof is the fact that my guilt is no longer there. I know my actions in the past, and all that has passed, have led me to where I am today and that where I am is where God wants me to be. My freewill may have made that journey tougher than it had to be, just as Merry's freewill may have as well, but I have no doubt my feet have landed where they were intended to go. That feeling of forgiveness, the lifting of my guilt, the feeling of being welcomed into a community, accepted as I am, was the warm hug from a friend I had hoped to feel. It was there. It was different than I expected. More than I expected. I did not expect forgiveness; a smarter man in God's ways may have, but I did not. The warm hug of that forgiveness was matched with a warm hug from Beth. I felt like hugging everyone in the church. I did grab a pastor, one of those "constellations," and gave him a hug too.

So a note of warning to the Christian community, my new community: *I have joined your ranks in a public admission of faith. I am blessed by God, full of questions, with eyes wide open and excited to be on this great adventure, the search for grace. Oh, and there's that hugging thing too, so you are fairly warned.*

CHAPTER 7.
ARRIVING WHEREVER

What I have tried to capture in this series of journal entries is how I have felt and thought during my grief experience. This experience changed me. It has changed how I view life, how I view God, and how I view death. I'll be the first to admit I do not have any answers. But what I have is faith. Much more so than I had before.

I do not know if death is final. I have no idea what happens to people when they die. Especially if they were, like Merry, genuinely "good" people but not church members. However, I believe God is a loving God. I believe God loved Merry and that she, her goodness, her spirit, her soul is at peace. I cannot say I believe death is final. After all, I heard her sing to me on that overpass. I still find that difficult to admit, but it is truth. Yes, I am certain some other, more rational explanation could be made, but does it matter? The effect is the same. That moment changed me. Whether it was Merry, my own mind, or divine intervention, at that moment I received permission to be happy. It is something I wish everyone could understand.

I do not know how God can be involved in every aspect of my life as an active participant, but I believe He/She/It/"God" is. God and gravity do share at least one thing:

just as gravity is often taken for granted, so is God, but both are always there.

I don't know how it all works. That great struggle between good and evil. Why God gave man freewill, and then seems forced to have to endure the pain of watching us make mistakes. Having to hear us blame him for what are often the results of our own poor choices. Having to hear us blame him for not doing what we want. Hearing us curse his name for not saving a relative or for not curing a friend. That freewill thing. It lets us be able to do that. Amazing how much love it must have taken for God to give us that gift, as God must have known what it would lead to. So even today I know I can choose to deny God. Even after publicly declaring my faith, and putting this much of myself into writing this journal, I know I have the freedom, given by God, to walk away from it and go back to believing God is like gravity, a non-caring, equally applied force. But just as saying no to cigarettes has eventually become my norm, so has saying yes to God. That freewill thing includes being able to choose either way.

I don't know anything about religion. I thought I knew. I thought I had a good base from my childhood Sunday school classes. Boy, was I wrong. There is so much that I either misunderstood or completely missed. Misgivings, misunderstanding, misplaced fears, and just plain arrogance caused me to back away from God. Yet He/She/It/God was patient. God continued to love me, even when I insisted on taking the wrong turns.

I don't know anything about how others experience grief except what I have read online and what I learned in the few grief counseling sessions I attended. What I do know is that I have done my best to capture my true feelings as I have lived through this.

I don't know where my relationship will lead with Beth. I know it is an adventure worth having. I believe she is one of those people God has put in my life to help me, or for us to help each other. Online, on the Internet, I have read what I think is a somewhat hurtful saying: "Women mourn, and men replace." It is based on statistical data no doubt and in my opinion, compiled by someone who has only observed others and never felt the direct loss of a spouse. A nicer way to phrase it may have been to say that women and men arrive at Wherever, Whenever by different routes.

In my feelings, there is no intention of replacing Merry. It simply could not be done. But I do know I want to replace the happiness I felt when sharing my life with someone I love. I know Beth makes me happy. We, Beth and I, know I am still grieving. That honesty thing isn't just in this writing that I try to use it, it is in everything. I always thought I was an honest person. But being honest at the emotional level, honestly answering the "How are you doing?" question and talking about those emotions is tough. It is new to a reformed introvert like me. I may never be great at it, but I now think it is important.

Today provided a good example. This morning, I felt "blah." I started out feeling good, but as the morning progressed, I felt I needed to apologize to Beth for not having fully discussed a couple of decisions I had made with her. Odd decisions, like deciding to learn to play the ukulele. So I apologized to her. Unnecessarily, according to her, since she was glad I had decided to learn a musical instrument. She didn't even comment on my choice of the ukulele. She was supportive, and I felt much better afterward. Even if the air was clear on her side, it wasn't on mine, so instead of letting it fester, I talked to her. Honesty, openness, vulnerability. They are not synonyms for weakness.

Finally, I don't know what God wants, except God wants us all to know his love, to trust in him, and to love him back. I do not know my purpose. I don't even know why I felt it important to write this. I just know that for me, it was. I have hope that it has a purpose. I hope it helps someone. It has already helped me. If someday this does get published or distributed, and you are reading it, I hope it makes you cry. Yes, as odd as that may sound, I hope you cry. Cry, and then find a person you love and tell that person you love him or her. If someone you love has died, take a minute and look around. Look for that person. I don't know what you will see. I hope you see your loved one, maybe as a dust storm swirling in an open field. Maybe as a butterfly settling on a flower or fluttering close to you. Maybe as a snowflake, or just in a familiar photograph. However it happens, I hope it does.

I hope you are reminded of their love and that you, like me when I remember Merry, remember the happiness they brought to your life. Remember them, and then say a prayer of thanks to God and go enjoy the day he has given you, Whenever, Wherever you may be.

PART FOUR.
IT ISN'T OVER TILL GRIEF SAYS IT IS OVER

journal entries after I thought I was through

CHAPTER 8.
GRIEF GETS A VOTE

You see, it would have been nice to end on that note; I accept Merry's death, I accept God into my life, and I issue a challenge to the world. *Hear me! Hear my voice, and know I am alive and know that even though I don't understand it all and undoubtedly never will, I am trying to be what God wants.* Yes, that would have been a good closing.

But that is not where this story ends. In retrospect, I think I have known this story could not end there, even while writing it. This story is about life and grief, and neither is that simple.

It is early December, and I am coming up on the anniversary of Merry's diagnosis. It all comes back as vividly as if it was yesterday. We had been playing golf, walking the front nine at a local course we had played many times. Merry noticed pain when she took a full, hard swing. That was the first time she felt like she needed to see a doctor. The next day, we went to the gym. Merry cut her run short, at forty-five minutes, saying she felt pain when she took a deep breath. Two days later we spent the night in the ER.

I remember those days, and each memory is a grief

surge. I cry more. I seem to have spent a lot of time crying in these past months.

But my memories are not the only thing I am dealing with. This month, December is not only Christmas but was also our wedding anniversary, and as you can gather from her name, "Merry," it was her birthday month. It is also my brother's birthday month and Beth's as well. I am torn between memories and grief, and moments and joy.

My brother. It was a peaceful Saturday night until the phone rang at 9:41 p.m. It was my brother's wife asking me to come over *now*! My brother was drunk and having flashbacks of his time in combat. I could hear him yelling in the background, and I went there as fast as I could.

My younger brother is a retired from the navy and was wounded during the second Iraq invasion. He is now classified as 100 percent disabled. He is on pain medications constantly, so alcohol mixing in is not a good idea. I believe he suffers from post-traumatic stress disorder (PTSD), and being stubborn and proud, he does not use the counseling services the Veterans Administration can provide. Another ingredient that makes for a bad alcohol cocktail.

Upon my arrival at his house, I was met by his wife, who had clearly been crying, but was mostly scared and angry. My brother was on his living room floor and had just vomited. He was rolling around in it, pounding his fist and yelling, "I don't want to kill anymore." I joined him there on the floor and hugged him to me hard. I told him he doesn't have to kill anymore. Those times are past now. I told him God loves him no matter what he had done during the war. I told him I loved him too. I held him there on the floor, in the puke, and told him those things over and over. "God loves you; no matter what, God loves you. I love you; you are my brother, and I love you." I held him for two hours before he recognized me and started to respond in some coherent fashion. He told me the things going through his head. Memories of death and tough decisions made with little information and no time. Memories of soldiers. Sorrow for families, sorrow for friends, sorrow for everyone impacted and anger, lots of anger at the politicians who brought the war.

We talked as soldiers can about war and pain and silence. We talked as brothers can about love and the things hidden in family closets. He began to sober up and grew more coherent as the night passed and the morning approached. We stood in his garage, in the cold air, and talked. Vomit-covered, cold, but not caring.

That night something important happened. Two brothers talked openly, honestly about life. Two soldiers confronted the horrors of memory. In the end, we gave it all up to God. All the pain of the memories, all the guilt over what was done, all the anger at the decision makers. We gave it to God. My brother had spent most of the night telling me the reasons he was justified in feeling guilty. He had seen the worst of war. He had made life or death decisions. How could he not feel guilty? I told him God knew what he had done and loved him anyway. I told him God can handle all of that guilt he feels; just give it to him.

Each time that guilt feeling comes up, remind himself that God has it and let God have it. I shared how Merry's loss had left me feeling guilty. Guilty for not being able to save her, failing somehow to keep her safe. Guilty for not having tried harder at getting her to know God. I told him I knew God had taken all of my guilt. I felt it leave on that Sunday morning when I took communion. As we talked, we remembered our childhood church. Something from those days was on his mind.

He told me he still very clearly remembered (even in his drunken, medicated, agitated state) one night when we attended a tent revival meeting as kids. The reverend ministered, and when the offering plate came by, my brother and I dumped the little money we had made from selling crawfish into the plate. It must have been a memorable sight. Two young boys, I think I was twelve and he was ten, no doubt dressed in dirty jeans and T-shirts, likely in need of haircuts, dropping our few dollars and cents into the plate. The reverend called us up on the platform, and we told him about how we had spent a couple days catching crawfish, cleaning them, and had sold them to a local hotel so they could make them into crawfish pie. We had found out about the opportunity somehow through our eldest sister, as I recall. Looking back it sounds like a Norman Rockwell painting or a chapter from *Tom Sawyer*.

The reverend prayed for us, and in the Pentecostal way, he laid hands on our heads. I have mentioned before that I often thought I was lacking something emotionally because I never felt much beyond confusion during my childhood church experiences. This was no exception for me. I remember feeling that the reverend was pressing very hard on my forehead and that my neck sort of hurt, but that was about it. My brother, on the other hand, fell out in the spirit. The reverend went on to proclaim he had a revelation that one of us two brothers would grow up to become a minister.

This was on my brother's mind. I had forgotten that tent revival, chalked it up to church theatrics. But he had taken it seriously and said it was one of the things he felt guilty over. Guilt that he had not heeded God's call to become a minister. Clearly, in his mind, since he had felt the Holy Spirit that night and I hadn't, he was the one destined to become a minister. He had no desire or intention to become a minister and felt guilty. He told me he thought I should become a minister so he wouldn't feel the need anymore. I laughed. I told him about this story. I am not sure it is the sort of "ministry" the reverend meant, but it seems close enough for me and I think that once my brother reads it, he will agree.

We hugged and told each other I love you. I left for my house for some much-needed sleep.

Sunday I picked up lunch and delivered it to my brother and his wife. We talked a bit about the previous night. I gave him a copy of this journal story on a thumb drive; then we dumped all of his alcohol down the drain.

Two days later we talked on the phone. I wanted to see how he was since I had been suffering from a cold since last seeing him. What I learned was that he had been suffering too, but from something much worse than a cold. He had gone to the VA doctor for a chest X-ray and was told they think he has pulmonary fibrosis. The prognosis is three to five years to live.

My brother is quite extraordinary. He feels more for

others than he does himself. His worry was how his wife was handling the bad news about his health. He too, it seems, is on mission. On a mission to take care of his loved ones, like I was with Merry. Maybe it is a trait of soldiers. Maybe it is a male thing. Maybe it is a universal trait among humans, that ability to worry more about others than ourselves at times. Or maybe it is just love.

I love my brother. I don't want this to happen to him. I don't want to lose him. Not even five years from now. This is not fair. This is tough. This hurts. I am not on a mission. I am sad. I am pitiful. I am mourning my brother before he even has a final diagnosis. Not waiting to find out what God has in store, just going straight to sad. Pitiful. I know better.

I pray: God, this is yours. God, your will be done. God, I put my trust in you knowing you love me and that you love my brother. Your will be done. Thank you for your love and for the opportunity to live in your grace. Amen.

Last year at this time I would not have said that prayer. Last year, if his wife had called me at 9:41 on a Saturday evening, I would probably not have gone to help. I would have probably told her to call 911 and get an ambulance for him. When I heard from my brother about his diagnosis, I would have told him that if there is anything I could do, just ask, but I would not have meant it. I would have said it knowing that he would not ask. I would have told myself that I had done the "Christian thing" by offering.

Today, I know that is wrong. Today, my heart hurts for my brother. He doesn't need to ask. I will help him and his family, period. I will pray for him and with him. Today, I have only some small understanding of God's grace, and much more to learn, but I do know that Love is the most important thing. God wants us to love one another. That means more than just answering the phone. It requires having enough love to get in the car, drive there, and hug your vomit-covered brother until the sun comes up. That's the kind of love I think God wants from us. I have no idea if I can love that much, but I will try. I am scared I cannot do it, but I will try.

I tried to put up Christmas decorations but could not do it. There are an amazing number of memories packed away in those boxes full of holiday decorations. Cards from friends, cards we gave each other, ornaments commemorating events and travels, and reminders of decorating and spending past Christmases together.

But the worst is remembering that this year is different; Merry is dead. The counseling provided from the hospice gave me some warning of this and also gave me some help. They recommended embracing those memories and this "different" Christmas by making a new custom of remembering Merry in some way. I had no idea how to do that or what was appropriate. I really didn't think I would need any help getting through this holiday season; after all, I have declared that I am in acceptance. Yeah, right. Grief gets a vote all to itself in these things. So, a caution, yes, the first time you experience a Christmas without your loved one, you will need help. Friends, family, church—all and any be advised and ready. I try to present a strong front, but Beth and a few close friends and neighbors see right through it, and frankly, I am very grateful they do. They simply remind me they are there, and that helps.

That reminds me I need to tell them all how much it helps and to thank them.

So as I began trying to decorate for Christmas, my question of what to do to remember Merry solved itself. I found that I simply could not put up any Christmas decorations in the house without first visiting her gravesite and doing a little decorating there as well. Yeah, it seems odd, but no doubt by the time you have read this far, you know that odd and I are not strangers. It felt good. It felt right to see the Christmas angel on Merry's headstone. Upon returning home, my decorating efforts may not have been superb (to anyone but me), but they were done in good spirits. This year's theme is angels.

The weather is not making me feel any better. My runs through the park have been few and far between. I have substituted gym visits, but I do miss running outdoors.

Merry's rapid decline and my brother's recent diagnosis have caused me to worry that at any minute, something horrible could happen to my own health. I worry at every cough whether it is serious or not. This paranoia only makes a medical problem I do have seem worse than it probably is. Yeah, surprise, right? One paragraph I am complaining that I cannot go out and run for a few hours in the park, and now I am opining that I have a medical problem I am growing more concerned about. Well, honesty, right? I have something called acute anal fissures. I think I have had them occasionally for most of my life, but since my bicycle trip they have been much worse than ever before. I had always written them off as occasional hemorrhoid flare-ups. I had never heard of anal fissures. I'll leave the descriptions up to the medical sites on the Internet. Suffice it to say they are very painful. In defense of bicycling, I should point out that my ride really had little to do with this condition, except that I let myself get dehydrated a few times, and that caused me to strain during bowel movements. That caused this flare-up. Not sure why it is not stopping, though, after now watching my diet (more fiber and more liquids) and using stool softeners every day along with prescription medications for seven months. Hence my paranoia. Seven months of pain that is not going away. Not much of a diagnosis and no currently planned changes to treatment. I am frustrated and getting worried, waiting for my doctor to refer me to a specialist. Dreading my doctor will refer me to a specialist. Is it cancer?

For those of you who are thinking, *You should just ask your doctor about your concerns and talk about treatment options,* I say ha! If you are thinking that sort of thing actually happens in the real world of today's routine doctor-patient relationships, you are believing too much in television advertising. It takes me three weeks to get an appointment to see my doctor. I made the mistake of telling the scheduler that I was suffering from a hemorrhoid flare-up as the reason for my first visit to get treatment for this problem. Sure enough, that's what the doctor treated me for. I spent a month making my anal fissures worse applying the prescribed creams that in essence restricted blood flow when I needed it to increase. Luckily I was scheduled for a colonoscopy at the end of that month and actually had an examination and a diagnosis of the problem. But, as I have mentioned, even that prescribed treatment doesn't seem to be working, so maybe it is wrong too. Okay, I'll get off my soapbox for now. But I can't promise that I won't boldly remount it at some point during the next three weeks while I await my next appointment. And while I watch my brother's diagnosis and treatment continue. While I worry, is this something serious? While I remember that Merry had six weeks from first symptom to funeral.

For a distraction and to make myself happier, I decided to organize a donation for my friend Peter's bike clinic. I have hit my friends up for donations of used bike parts, new tubes, bicycle locks and cables, tires, brake pads, and patch kits as well as for gloves and knit caps. I don't know anything about being homeless, but I have spent a few nights out in the cold during my army days. Wool caps and good gloves are a necessity, bicycling or not.

On this date last year, Merry and I were back in the ER wrestling with breakthrough pain. Breakthrough pain is the description for when a patient's pain becomes too intense for their pain medications to relieve it. Excruciating for the person in pain. A helpless feeling for those close to them. Nothing to do but go to the ER, hold hands, and wait for the docs and pharmacists. I hate it. I hate the feeling; I hate remembering how it felt to see her in pain. How it felt to know she was slipping away more and more. The fear at how fast the cancer was progressing. The anger and injustice. The memory eases off, replaced by anger at the disease. I say a prayer that God will give strength to those in pain and to those trying to help them. I remind myself to leave the past in the past and live in today.

Well, my own health worries continue. I did see a

doctor, but really no help. A quick look at the problem area, a prescription for hydrocortisone cream, pain medication, and a referral to a surgeon (to be seen another few weeks from now). So it looks like this "different" Christmas will be one with physical as well as emotional pain. Dang. This is no fun. I feel like I have complained so much to Beth and to my friends that they are tired of hearing it. I know I am tired of it. I read back through my Facebook posts and am embarrassed at their tone. Angry rants have become my norm, it appears. I will have to watch that. While the occasional rant may be good for clearing the mind, doing so constantly seems depressing. Social media can also be a way to spread good feelings and encouragement to friends. I should be telling my friends about the good things, not venting about things I have no control over, and in the long run, really are not important. I can blame it on being in pain, but that does not make it right.

I think I will post the following: "Friends, posting an apology for venting. It dawns on me that although politics and the state of our nation are popular discussion items, I can change neither thing in any great measure, especially not by ranting about them on Facebook. However, what I can do to improve the world is this: I can simply be a positive voice, not a ranter. All I need to do is remember the important things—love, honesty, humor, and charity. Especially at this time of year. So, I humbly apologize."

Christmas (Merry's birthday) arrived and passed. I kept busy. I deliberately did not think about a year ago, when it was Merry's last good day. I spent the day with Beth and her children. They shared their love and joy with me. We had a fun time. A traditional Christmas: torn wrapping paper scattered everywhere, too many things to enjoy at once. New games to play and learn, a beehive of pajama-clad activity ending with a ham dinner.

But today, the day after, is different. Today, I am alone. Today, a year ago was the first of the "no more good days" for Merry, and I began this unwanted journey. I began my day today by trying to be busy, putting away gifts, taking down a few decorations, chatting with Beth online, but I haven't been able to get away from it. I sat down and read some in the new Bible Beth gave me for Christmas. Normally a comfort, but today the grief surges over me like waves. Grief, it seems, gets a vote each moment in my life still.

The next few weeks lead up to where this story began, that day I took Merry into the hospice. The coming days will no doubt each bring a memory of some event that passed a year before. But there is no stopping the calendar. Those days will pass, some with tears, some with smiles. Eventually, when enough days have passed, I will truly arrive at Whenever, Wherever. I know God will be with me on that journey.

CHAPTER 9.
ENDINGS

expect to live a long Life (with a capital "L"). Along with that expectation, though, I am acutely aware that in doing so, others I love will die before I do. Perhaps my brother, given his current prognosis, but there is no way of knowing. God may not yet plan to call him home. I dread the thought of having to grieve for him, or for anyone. It is an emotionally painful process. This experience has taught me that grief is unavoidable, though. We cannot love and be mortal without experiencing grief at some point. I hope that what I have shared in this journal helps in some way to prepare us all for those times. As for myself, when it does come time for people to grieve for me, I would want them to know this: I have been blessed by God my whole life. Yes, there were times I doubted it. Even times I forgot it. But God has always been there for me, active in everything, every moment of my life, just as he is in yours. The loss of a love from life causes a void. God's love is there to fill that void.

So when my days are over a long time from now (God willing), know that any void I leave behind will be filled with something better. Remember me, just as I remember the loved ones I have lost; have a good long cry, laugh at my odd life, and then thank God for the blessings in your life.

From the wreckage, one figure emerged. Smoke and flames swirled; twisted metal landed with loud crashes all around. The shrapnel flew high and pieces rained down in a seemingly endless falling. Yet the figure walked on. Feeling his way, step by step, crashing into a hot, sharp piece of wreckage here, getting caught by a falling shard there, blinded by the smoke, but onward, out of the wreckage. The train wreck was a spectacle, but what happened afterward was the real story. The figure felt the heat, felt the pain, and was broken but not crushed. He was perplexed but did not despair. He was struck down but not destroyed (2 Corinthians 4). Shrouded in God's love, his eyes fixed not on what was seen but on what is unseen, since what is seen is temporary, but what is unseen is eternal. The figure walked on. On the way to Wherever, Whenever.

"A POEM FOR MERRY"

Ronnie Lee Graham

Remember me and shed your tears.
I too will miss you in the passing years.
Remember me, full of life.
Recall my joy to lessen your strife.
Our adventures continue, apart for now.
We'll share a path again, when time will allow.

    The video "Merry Travels" is on YouTube. I watch it and remember Merry. This is the end of this selection of journal entries, but Life (full of Love) continues.

CPSIA information can be obtained at www.ICGtesting.com
Printed in the USA
LVOW10s1401081014

407848LV00001B/3/P